Advance Praise for

Misogyny in English Departments

"This book is a ground-breaking contribution to the English discipline, promising to change the very way in which English faculty members understand the work that we do. Casting bright light from the MeToo Movement directly upon academia—Robillard reveals the insidious ways in which some of the most supposedly 'enlightened' spaces, English Departments, often depend upon very disturbing misogynistic cultural practices. She couples meticulous, complex analyses and research with a voice that is simply stunning—always clear, always candid, and always calling the guilty to account. Robillard's must-read book should be prominently displayed on all English Department's faculty lounge coffee tables and discussed repeatedly at our faculty meetings. It should also serve as a crucial model for other academic disciplines that desperately need to do similar sorts of self-reflection."

—Laura A. Gray-Rosendale, President's Distinguished Teaching Fellow and Professor of English, Northern Arizona University; Author of *College Girl: A Memoir*, and Editor of *Me Too, Feminist Theory, and Surviving Sexual Violence in the Academy*

"*Misogyny in English Departments* meticulously and empathetically documents women's experiences with misogyny across ranks and positions in English Departments. Many of us will recognize our experiences with misogyny on these pages and in the voices of Robillard's interviewees. The interviewees have generously and courageously shared their stories and mapped the toll that misogyny has taken on their work lives, bodies, and psyches. In an age where universities and departments proclaim diversity, equity, and inclusion initiatives, Robillard calls out misogyny as 'the law enforcement branch of patriarchy' and demonstrates how women are often policed, punished, overworked, undervalued, and dismissed in English Departments. This book makes an important contribution to critiques of gendered labor structures and feminist analyses of sexual harassment and sex discrimination. Robillard and the interviewees' analyses of misogynistic patterns and logics give us frameworks for calling out and fighting those patterns in our English Departments and Writing Programs."

—Eileen E. Schell, Professor of Writing and Rhetoric and Faculty Affiliate in Women's and Gender Studies, Syracuse University

Misogyny in English Departments

Beth Powers-Costello
GENERAL EDITOR

vol. 17

The Equity in Higher Education Theory, Policy, & Praxis series
is part of the Peter Lang education list.
Every volume is peer reviewed and meets
The highest quality standards for content and production.

PETER LANG
New York • Berlin • Brussels • Lausanne • Oxford

Amy E. Robillard

Misogyny in English Departments

Obligation, Entitlement, Gaslighting

PETER LANG
New York • Berlin • Brussels • Lausanne • Oxford

Library of Congress Cataloging-in-Publication Data
Names: Robillard, Amy E., author.
Title: Misogyny in English departments: obligation, entitlement,
gaslighting / Amy E. Robillard.
Description: New York: Peter Lang, 2023. | Series: Equity in higher
education theory, policy, and praxis, Vol. 17 |
ISSN 2330-4502 (print) | ISSN 2330-4510 (online)
Includes bibliographical references and index.
Identifiers: LCCN 2022060397 (print) | LCCN 2022060398 (ebook) | ISBN
9781433199578 (paperback) | ISBN 9781433199585 (hardback) | ISBN
9781433197208 (ebook) | ISBN 9781433197215 (epub)
Subjects: LCSH: Sex discrimination in higher education—United States. |
Sexual harassment in universities and colleges—United States. | Women
college teachers—Professional relationships—United States. | English
language—Study and teaching (Higher)—Social aspects—United States. |
Misogyny—United States.
Classification: LCC LC212.862. R63 2023 (print) | LCC LC212.862 (ebook) |
DDC 378.0082—dc23/eng/20221219
LC record available at https://lccn.loc.gov/2022060397
LC ebook record available at https://lccn.loc.gov/2022060398
DOI 10.3726/b20558

Bibliographic information published by **Die Deutsche Nationalbibliothek**.
Die Deutsche Nationalbibliothek lists this publication in the "Deutsche
Nationalbibliografie"; detailed bibliographic data are available
on the Internet at http://dnb.d-nb.de/.

© 2023 Peter Lang Publishing, Inc., New York
80 Broad Street, 5th floor, New York, NY 10004
www.peterlang.com

All rights reserved.
Reprint or reproduction, even partially, in all forms such as microfilm,
xerography, microfiche, microcard, and offset strictly prohibited.

I dedicate this book to the women who shared their stories with me.
Thank you, truly.

"If you are silent about your pain, they'll kill you and say you enjoyed it."

—Zora Neale Hurston

"The task of incorporating women's experiences into our shared understanding of the world is giant. It is painful. It asks us to reorder all our priorities, all our understandings. It asks us to revisit our memories of times that we thought were placid or happy and to realize that they may in fact have been brutal."

—Moira Donegan

Contents

Foreword by Malea Powell		xi
Preface		xv
Acknowledgments		xix
Introduction: The Isolation of Misogyny		1
1	Silencing Women's Voices in Academic Spaces	27
2	The Expectation to Serve and Care for Others	43
3	Masculine-Coded Goods in English Departments: Respect, Authority, Leadership	57
4	Sexual Harassment and Women's Credibility	77
5	On Gaslighting	93
6	Women No Longer Want to Give	111
7	Less Precarious Stories	129
	Index	137

Foreword
Malea Powell

I'm not going to be coy. I love this book, and I admire both Robillard's research ethics and the incredibly useful theoretical and methodological pathways she walks as her participants' stories are shared with you here. Because of the many truths that get spoken here, my experience as a reader of this often felt both like an act of solidarity (the margins of my manuscript copy are covered with "Yesss!" and "OMFG") and like an act of shared mourning.

Like her participants, when I first heard about Robillard's plan for this project, I started nodding my head in agreement. It's often seemed ironic and irritating to me that even in the most so-called liberal, progressive, and justice-oriented English/humanities departments, there's an undercurrent of petty misogyny that works under the radar. Of course, these kinds of entitlement practices are what, as Robillard argues, uphold patriarchal systems within the university and persistently create more pressure for women to comply with those patriarchal norms or face punishment in those spaces. After all, misogyny, like racism, is a system, a social structure, in which the actions of specific "bad" individuals are often blamed while the entire class of individuals (in this case, men and women who "behave" correctly) continue to benefit from the structure/system. And we internalize misogyny, just like we internalize racism.

Like the individuals interviewed for this book, and like many of you reading this right now, I've lived these experiences (as well as other racist and colonialist experiences) for my entire 33+ years as an academic. I've been that person who complains, that person who "just sees oppression everywhere," that person who colleagues dismiss because I decided not to play the game. And I've lived the consequences. I'm not unique, though. So many of us have lived these stories and have lived the consequences of being seen as "complainers." As Robillard herself points out in the Preface (drawing from Ahmed), to be seen a making a complaint is to neither be seen nor heard authentically. Complaining about injustice, oppression, harassment make the complainer the "problem" to be solved to most department chairs and university administrators because the entire mechanism of the university was built to uphold the things that so many of us might be complaining about—white supremacy, patriarchy, heterosexist privilege, ableist privilege. So to complain about the "petty" and mundane behaviors being used to uphold those privileges is to make oneself a problem, an outsider, a gossip, someone who isn't collegial or a "team" player, someone who is selfishly thinking about themselves instead of the good of the unit/department/college/university. I am delighted with the way that Robillard allows her participants' stories to illuminate how these behaviors—from seemingly small acts like "hepeating" to larger crimes like outright sexual harassment—structure not just the experiences of women in specific academic spaces but how they accumulate to create and maintain specifically patriarchal cultures across different kinds of academic workspaces.

As you read these stories, I know they will remind you of your own stories, and of so many other stories of other ways that many of our experiences are belittled and erased. Hold all of those stories close and keep them warm. They are only one of our defenses in such an inhumane system, but they are a critical one. More importantly, remember, Robillard isn't just offering the stories told by her participants as another way to simply "name and blame" the acts of perpetrators and those who benefit from the entitlements of patriarchal oppression. Instead, Robillard asks us, her readers, to act as a community of colleague and scholars. She asks us to listen, to be thoughtful, to take responsibility, and to do things differently moving forward. She treats us as colleagues who might just be able to listen to what we've been doing badly and just might be able to put our heads together to do things in a better, more equitable way. In doing this, Robillard actually opens a window to hope, which seems like a radical act during a time when hope is increasingly hard to come by. For Robillard's work in honoring her participants' stories, in presenting them to us with such care, for asking us to look our own uglinesses right in the face, and for doing so in a way that charts a path to the possibility of creating spaces that are decidedly more thoughtful and equitable, I am grateful.

Preface

I've had enough. If someone is asking for my story, I'm telling it.

—Alyssa, associate professor

The stories that follow are tales told out of school. They break the rules we've all internalized about what we can and cannot tell, about what we should and should not tell, and they bust open the comfortable beliefs many of us continue to carry with us about equity in the academy. But for those of us who have experienced misogyny in our departments, the only thing busting open is the "expectation that you'll maintain this façade that everything is fine, that no one's racist, that no one's sexist, or any of those things," as one of my interviewees put it. The women I spoke with for this project are no longer conforming to that expectation, as they've decided that it's more important to tell their stories than it is to maintain that façade. The façade has done enough damage.

My goal in writing this book is not to persuade readers who do not already believe that misogyny exists in English departments; rather, my goal is to provide a resource for those who already understand that it does. Stories function as resources for other stories, and when we read the stories of others, we become more able and willing to tell our own stories. We see our experiences differently. We become able to name them in ways we perhaps hadn't been able to before. I want you to feel seen in these stories. I want you to understand that, when you are asked to care too much or to give too much at work, and when you are punished for not caring enough or not giving enough, that is misogyny. Though misogyny can be, of course, extreme, it is not always, and it is those less-than-extreme instances of misogyny that accumulate over the years, over a career, to become, as more than one of my interviewees noted, "death by a thousand cuts."

I came to this project after experiencing and witnessing misogyny in my own department, and I knew I was not alone. A lifelong carer of and teller of stories, I wanted to know more about how other women who had experienced and witnessed similar instances of misogyny reconciled—or not—their experiences with their departments' and discipline's commitment to equity, diversity, inclusion, and social justice. For me, the hypocrisy was startling at times, depressing at others, but always front and center. It was especially notable to me when, during a department meeting when we were discussing the possibility of evaluating faculty on the extent to which our teaching met diversity goals, one of the strongest women in our department was pushed to tears by the gaslighting she experienced from three men she sat on a committee with. She called out the gaslighting then and there, for which I was grateful, but department leadership responded by not responding. There were no repercussions for gaslighting a colleague in full view of the entire department. It was then that I decided that I needed to write this book, that I needed to collect more stories.

As I began interviewing, I anticipated the need to care for women's stories, to listen rhetorically and with empathy, to act as a responsible and ethical witness to the stories they were willing to share with me. Indeed, as I listened to participants' stories, I tried to become what Sara Ahmed calls a "feminist ear." "To hear with a feminist ear is to hear who is not heard, how we are not heard. If we are taught to tune out some people, then a feminist ear is an achievement" (*Complaint!* 4). A few women told me harrowing stories, stories that will stick with me for a very long time. Many women told me stories of trauma, and I listened to those with great care and have tried to represent them here ethically. Some women shared stories from a year earlier and some shared stories from decades ago. Because I was doing a project on misogyny in English departments, the women I interviewed came to me with an understanding that I would sympathize with their situations, and they were thus able to break down the walls they'd built around their stories. As one woman put it, while talking to me, "you're not going to be seeing as someone who's complaining. You're not gonna be seen as someone who instigated it or that it's your fault. Even though that's the way we're made to feel." As Ahmed writes in the opening lines of her new book, *Complaint!*, "To be heard as complaining is not to be heard. To hear someone as complaining is an effective way of dismissing someone. You do not have to listen to the content of what she is saying if she is *just* complaining or *always* complaining" (1). Many of the women

I spoke with were aware of how they sounded; they assured me they weren't just airing grievances, that they understood that they might sound like gossips, but also that such rhetoric is useful for the patriarchy to silence them. I assured each person I spoke with that I wanted to hear more, not less, of what they had to say, and that I understood that what they were telling me constituted experiences of distress and trauma. To hear with a feminist ear is to listen to stories the patriarchy considers dangerous.

One thing I could not have anticipated as I interviewed the women you'll meet in these pages is just how much laughter we shared. Sometimes, misogyny is patently absurd to the point where you cannot help but laugh about it. One brief example: There's the woman who sent an email to one interviewee's entire department about my interviewee's lack of fitness as a parent and a teacher. The email started out in French with a line in the beginning that said "only educated people know French," and my interviewee noted with sarcasm that we all know how to use Google translate, which she did, of course, to find that her colleague had written "two paragraphs in French about how every who's educated should know French or Latin, some rambling thing about how French is the language of the gods." And then the email continued to criticize my interviewee's parenting and teaching. In *French*! You cannot make this stuff up. Sometimes women laughed even as I was asking my questions because they understood what I was getting at, because they had so many things they wanted to share, because it was too obvious, for instance, the ways women are encouraged to deliver feminine-coded goods in their departments. "You can't see this, but I'm starting to smirk while you're asking your question. Oh, so many ways. So, so many ways," one woman said.

I listened, we laughed, and then I went away and transcribed the interviews myself, hearing things in the recordings that I hadn't noticed the first time, making notes as I went, and coming to appreciate my own skill as an interviewer. So many of us have said at one point or another how much we hate to hear our own voices; listening to myself interview thirty-nine women about their experiences with misogyny helped me not only become comfortable with my own voice, but come to like it. I then worked with the interview transcripts, sorting and categorizing and reorganizing their stories into chapters that morphed as I continued to see different themes. I read and reread those transcripts dozens of times, and I came to know these stories almost as well as I know my own. I came to love them. My gratitude for their trust in me grew each time I reread their stories, and I knew I had to present their stories with care.

This book foregrounds the voices of women. I have tried to cite as few men as possible, and I have put women's voices front and center. I am in this book, of course, as organizer, as interviewer, as commentator, but the book belongs to my interviewees. These are their stories. These are your stories. I hope you will find solace in them.

References

Ahmed, Sara. *Complaint!* Durham: Duke University Press, 2021.

Acknowledgments

As ever, Ron Fortune and Sarah Hochstetler listened to my ideas for this book and championed them from the beginning; I treasure you both. I learned so very much from the women I interviewed for this project, and none of this would have been possible without your willingness to take the risk of speaking out. For that, I thank you sincerely. To all of my colleagues and friends who shared the call for participants, I offer my gratitude. And finally, to my husband, Steve, and our beautifully mischievous dogs, thank you, thank you. You are my light.

Introduction: The Isolation of Misogyny

There is always something unsaid and yet to be said, always someone struggling to find the words and the will to tell her story. Every day each of us invents the world and the self who meets that world, opens up or closes down space for others within that. Silence is forever being broken, and then like waves lapping over the footprints, the sandcastles and washed-up shells and seaweed, silence rises again.

—Rebecca Solnit, "A Short History of Silence"

It's not gonna get better if we're quiet. We're just gonna die quietly.

—Interview participant

Only recently have I come to understand that the family I grew up in disciplined my responses to stimuli in ways that have had long-term effects. I was told not to cry when I was sad or hurt. I was told that I had no right to be angry when, in fact, I did. I was told that my capacity for irritation was simply wrong. I was, in other words, expected to be a cardboard cutout and not a person. It struck me recently that this education in how to feel and how not to feel—in how to *respond* to the world around me—has shaped my persistent interest in the ways those who are abused are blamed not just for being abused but for *telling* about their abuse. It is the very fact of the telling that so often gets pointed to as the problem, the teller being characterized as a whiner or a tattletale or a gossip or a big old baby. At the same time that I am confounded by this—isn't the original abuse the real problem here?—I also get it. If we don't *hear about* the original abuse, we can all simply pretend that it never happened.

Others have pointed to this phenomenon in much more eloquent ways than I. Rebecca Solnit, in her essay, "A Short History of Silence," writes,

> One disturbing aspect of abuse and harassment is the idea that it's not the crime that's the betrayal but the testimony about the crime. You're not supposed to tell. Abusers often assume this privilege that demands the silence of the abused, that a nonreciprocal protection be in place. Others often impose it as well, portraying

the victims as choosing to ruin a career or a family, as though the assailant did not make that choice himself. (40)

Even more to the point than Solnit, though, is David Graeber in his essay, "The Bully's Pulpit." In working through the reasons why grade school kids stand by passively in the face of bullying, Graeber notes that one reason may be that they have "caught on to how adult authority operates and mistakenly assume the same logic applies to interactions with their peers." Graeber continues, "The fates of the Mannings and the Snowdens of the world are high-profile advertisements for a cardinal rule of American culture: while abusing authority may be bad, openly pointing out that someone is abusing authority is much worse—and merits the severest punishment." We need only point to Anita Hill and Christine Blasey Ford for more evidence of this phenomenon; speaking out about the abuse we have experienced more often than not leads to more abuse.

We are effectively being told to shut up.

I want you to know now what I will be arguing throughout this book: dealing with the misogyny that others deny even exists in English departments takes crucial time away from women's lives and academic work. It is exhausting, unhealthy, and time-consuming. Even talking about the misogyny they experience is exhausting because women anticipate being characterized as liars, as gossips, as untrustworthy before they even begin to tell. But they talked to me. And I'm incredibly grateful that they did because they have allowed me to share with you the stories that make up what follows.

In the summer of 2019, I spoke with thirty-nine women who work in English departments across the United States about their experiences with misogyny in the workplace. My goal in these interviews was to understand women's experiences of misogyny in their departments, the effects of such misogyny on their work and personal lives, and the ways such a focus on *women's experiences* of misogyny—as opposed to the usual approach to the naïve conception of misogynists—might help those of us working in English departments specifically and the academy more generally see more clearly the way our everyday interactions reinforce patriarchal norms of obligation and entitlement. Of the thirty-nine women I interviewed, ten were doctoral students, five were assistant professors, eight were associate professors, eight were full professors, seven were non-tenure-track instructors, and one was an emerita professor. Three women were department chairs. Twenty-two women identified their subfield as rhetoric and composition or writing studies, six as literature, six as creative writing, two as children's literature, two as linguistics, and one as English and theater. Four women taught in a community college, ten in a Research-1 university, twenty in a Research-2 university, four in four-year colleges, and one in a HBCU. The average age of interviewees was 43. I did not ask interviewees to identify their race or ethnicity, though I did ask them to reflect on the extent to which they believed their race, ethnicity, sexuality, ability, and/or religion contributed to their experiences of misogyny in their departments. All participation in the study was voluntary and confidential; though I know participants' names, the nature of this research demands that participants' names and institutions be kept confidential.

I investigated misogyny in English departments because English departments market themselves as spaces of equity and diversity, as dedicated to inclusivity and social justice, as committed to rooting out injustices like misogyny via such means as socially just, feminist, and critical pedagogies. We are some of the very people who teach students to recognize and fight back against social injustices like misogyny, so to acknowledge that it is happening among us faculty is to acknowledge, on some level, a failure. It is to acknowledge a failure on the part of the culture of academia broadly and English departments specifically, to recognize and to resist the norms of patriarchy among ourselves.[1] Misogyny in English departments is not more important or more egregious than misogyny in other spaces, but it is important enough to warrant attention, for it has received almost none.

In the era of #MeToo and Kavanaugh, we in English departments, and writing studies especially, are just beginning to publicly share our stories of sexual harassment and bullying. Until very recently, we had more stories of bullying than we had of sexual harassment, and we still have incredibly few stories of misogyny that do not fall under the category of sexual harassment. In the last decade or so, scholars in the humanities and social sciences have begun asking questions about what constitutes a bully culture (Twale and De Luca) and how we might understand the causes of and learn ways to prevent bullying (Twale). In English Studies specifically, Cristyn L. Elder and Bethany Davila address the

---

1   I want to be clear that, as a member of said academy and as a member of an English department, I am complicit in misogyny. I am working to become more aware of the ways I differentiate between good women and bad women based on the extent to which they conform to the norms of patriarchy. And I am becoming more aware of the ways I try to conform so as to avoid the punishments that are likely to follow. This work began in my own experiences of misogyny, but it doesn't end there; it stretched to include and try to understand the experiences of others who have had similar experiences.

culture of silence that surrounds bullying in the academy and frame such abuse as a social justice issue as they examine the intricacies of bullying in writing programs. Importantly, Elder and Davila address the issue of riskiness in the introduction to their collection when they write, "When we issued the CFP for this collection, we were struck by how many people contacted us directly to thank us for taking on this work and often to express regret at not being able to contribute, given the possibility for retribution on their campuses" (4). Because of the large number of people who felt they could not contribute for fear of retaliation, Elder and Davila take the extraordinary step of including a blank chapter at the end of the collection, entitled "'I Can't Afford to Lose My Job': A Chapter Dedicated to All Those Who Found It Too Risky to Contribute." The chapter is authored by Anonymous and the entire content of the chapter is "We reserve this space for them" (190).

In *Sexual Harassment and Cultural Change in Writing Studies*, Patricia Freitag Ericsson argues that it is our job "to make trouble for those who carry and spread this toxic disease" (viii), and she points out that "despite this field's concern about a variety of social issues, a similar concern about sexual harassment has been sorely missing" (6). In her introduction to *Composition Studies'* 2018 Where We Are section focused on #MeToo and academia, Laura Micciche characterizes the pieces to follow as

> infuriating and depressing; we need them. We need more of them. Those of us who have been in the field of rhetoric and composition for a while now know stories of serial harassers whose careers flourish unfettered. We've heard stories passed discreetly among friends at conferences and in hallways. Yet the number of submissions we received for this section didn't break double digits, and the majority of submissions came from those with the least power in our field: graduate students and non-tenure-track faculty. Few addressed peer-to-peer violence and harassment, an open secret in the field (and in academia more widely).

In that Where We Are section, seven women share their stories of gendered violence, and only one, Anne Sicari, addresses the issue of peer-to-peer violence when she writes, "we need to reflect on our everyday practices, on how we treat our colleagues and students, and ways in which we perpetuate patriarchal ideologies regularly, without much thought" (201). Katelyn Lusher articulates what I imagine many of us once felt when she writes, "When I began grad school, I had a somewhat utopian belief that most professors were so 'woke' they couldn't possibly subscribe to the misogyny I had felt in so many workplaces. What I quickly learned was that barely disguised sexism and harassment are as much a part of academia as conferences, publishing, and happy hours that go far into the night" (199). We are talking, as a field, about sexual harassment and bullying, but not about misogyny more generally, and when we talk about sexual harassment, we talk primarily about it in terms of breaches of the teacher/mentor and student relationship. I join these scholars to ask why we're not sharing stories about misogyny more broadly between peers—faculty-to-faculty and graduate student-to-graduate student.

This work matters because in our field, there is not a single scholarly consideration of women's experiences of misogyny understood as the systematic punishment of women for not *caring enough*, for not *giving enough*; that is what this work contributes. Though it is of course true that women also experience intersectional oppression, my focus here is on how those who identify as women experience misogyny in English departments. This leaves much work to be done, and I hope other researchers will investigate class, race, ability, sexuality, and religion as axes across which misogyny is compounded.

In the rest of this Introduction, I will provide an overview of my working understanding of misogyny, drawing on Kate Manne's work in *Down Girl: The Logic of Misogyny*. I will then describe my methodology, which I characterize as building a collective of stories against a backdrop of the concepts of precarious narratives and narrative habitus. I follow that section with a consideration of the risks women took in sharing their stories with me, and I finish this Introduction with an overview of the rest of the book.

Misogyny: Enforcing Patriarchal Norms

I want to be explicit about how I am defining misogyny, and the best way for me to do that is to draw from the work that animates and motivates this work: Kate Manne's *Down Girl: The Logic of Misogyny*. The commonplace understanding many people have of misogyny is as a psychological characteristic of individual people, usually men, who hate women—all women—simply because they are women. The problem with this naïve conception of misogyny is that it centers the experiences of the individual agent rather than the target of misogyny and it makes *identifying* misogyny all but impossible, as any individual man can point to the women in his life and claim to love them, thus negating the label of misogynist. This is an old story. Rather, the new story that Manne tells in her crucial work is that misogyny "ought to be understood as the system that operates within a patriarchal social order to police and enforce women's subordination and to uphold male dominance" (33). To my mind, the most significant features of Manne's theorization of misogyny are the following:

1. In contrast to the naïve conception of misogyny, which targets women "because they are women in a *man's mind*, where that man is a misogynist," misogyny "primarily targets women because they are women in a *man's world* (i.e., a historically patriarchal one, among other things)." (64).
2. Because misogyny is systemic and political, the best way to understand it is to examine women's *experiences* of misogyny: "when it comes to misogyny, we can focus on the hostility women *face* in navigating the social world, rather than the hostility men…may or may not *feel* in their encounters with certain women—as a matter of deep psychological explanations, or indeed whatsoever" (59).
3. Misogyny is differentiated from sexism by a matter of degree. Where sexism discriminates "*between* men and women, typically by alleging sex differences beyond what is known or could be known," misogyny "will typically differentiate between good women and *bad* women and punishes the latter" (79). Where sexism should be understood as the "justificatory branch of a patriarchal order" (79), misogyny "should be understood primarily as the 'law enforcement' branch of a patriarchal order, which has the overall function of *policing* and *enforcing* its governing norms and expectations" (78).
4. Those primary governing norms and expectations of patriarchy have to do with *obligation* on the part of women and *entitlement* on the part of men. Women are obligated to *give* and men are entitled to *take*, to *receive*. She is obligated to give feminine-coded goods and services such as attention, affection, care, moral support, admiration, loyalty, and respect. He is entitled to take these and to receive masculine-coded goods such as "leadership, authority, influence, money, and other forms of power, as well as social status, prestige, rank, and the markers thereof. Then there are the less tangible facets of social 'face,' pride, reputation, or standing, and the relevant *absences*—for example, the freedom from shame and lack of public humiliation, which are more or less universally desired but only some people feel entitled to" (113). The norms, then, are: *"Don't ask for or take the kind of thing you're meant to be giving, either to him or to society"* (emphasis added; 112) and *"Don't ask for or try to take masculine-coded perks and privileges, at least as long as he desires them"* (emphasis added; 113).

5. Should a woman violate these patriarchal norms—by failing to care enough, by failing to be attentive enough, by seeking attention for herself—misogyny will punish her with any number of down-girl moves: "to generalize, adults are insultingly likened to children, people to animals or even to objects. As well as infantilizing and belittling, there's ridiculing, humiliating, mocking, slurring, vilifying, demonizing, as well as sexualizing or, alternatively *desexualizing*, silencing, shunning, blaming, patronizing, condescending, and other forms of treatment that are dismissive and disparaging in specific social contexts. Then there is violence and threatening behavior: including 'punching down'—that is, deferred or displaced aggression" (68).
6. Because misogyny is a self-masking phenomenon, "a misogynist social environment may but need not be the product of individual agents' bigotry." Rather, Manne explains that people may be responding, unknowingly, to their internal discomfort with the flouting of norms. "For some people, feminism in particular has profoundly disrupted their sense of the social order. The hostility they display to women who disrupt or pose a threat to gendered social hierarchies, say, is compatible with their being egalitarians in the abstract. They may nevertheless perceive powerful women who do not wield their power in service of men's interests as abrasive and threatening. For that reason among others, a misogynist social environment may be partly the result of more or less well-intentioned people acting out of disavowed emotions, or exhibiting flashes of aggression that are not consciously experienced" (61). A misogynist social environment may flourish, in other words, in spaces like academia, where so many of us consider ourselves egalitarian but are also committed to gendered social hierarchies in ways we may not even be conscious of.
7. Finally, because misogyny is the law enforcement wing of patriarchy, policing and punishing women who violate norms of giving and taking, misogyny is not restricted to men punishing women. Women who benefit from patriarchy will work to reinforce its norms as openly—or as covertly—as men.

Misogyny is perhaps best understood metaphorically this way: "like a shock collar used to keep dogs behind an invisible fence, misogyny, [Manne] argues, aims to keep women—those who are well trained as well as those who are unruly—in line" (Penaluma). One of the effects of Manne's conception of misogyny is that we who examine its workings in different environments do not have to understand what motivates the people who do and say the things we characterize as misogynistic. What matters, instead, is that women are experiencing hostility for their violation of patriarchal norms that we would claim, when given the opportunity, are gendered and problematic. Yet we enforce them, knowingly or not. And we enforce them at the expense of creating working environments that value the contributions of all of their members, a goal I imagine many of our department mission statements reference in one form or another.

Methodology: Building a Collective

The questions I posed to interviewees focused on their perceptions of gender roles in their departments, their perceptions of the norms of patriarchy in their departments—e.g., the extent to which women are obligated to deliver feminine-coded goods such as attention, affection, care, empathy, and loyalty—their experiences of misogyny, the effects of misogyny on their personal and professional lives, and their experiences reporting on misogyny in their departments and universities. I also asked participants why they chose to talk with me, and I analyze their responses to that question in the next section of this Introduction.

My methodology builds on my theorizing, in my earlier work, *We Find Ourselves in Other People's Stories*, of the concept of precarious narratives. In that work, I draw on Judith Butler's concept of precarious life and on Arthur Frank's insight that "stories are formed from other stories" ("Tricksters" 186) to propose that all narratives are precarious because their "circulation *relies fundamentally on social and political conditions*, [their] structures and themes must be *supported by what is outside itself*. These are the narrative resources upon which we draw when we tell the stories of our lives" (emphasis in original 29–30). Narrative resources are the necessary plotlines, character types, cultural scripts, and so on, that we all draw upon when we tell any kind of story; we can see with this concept that narratives are socially dependent, "needing support from other people and other narratives lest they collapse" (29). Narratives, like lives, are differentially precarious. A narrative becomes particularly precarious when its support is in question; a narrative becomes more precarious when others do not tell the same kind of story or when others question the truth value of one's story. If a precarious narrative requires support, requires propping up, then *others sharing similar stories* expands the possible narrative resources from which to create and share additional stories. As I write in *We Find Ourselves*,

If access to stories offers opportunities to figure out who we are and who we can become because the stories we create for ourselves are dependent on those narrative resources, recognizing that narratives are precarious should encourage us to tell the stories that challenge dominant cultural scripts. Thus, telling stories is important not just because it is empowering or because it provides an opportunity for silenced voices to be heard or because it helps us develop form from chaos but because *our stories and other's stories are interdependent.* They work together to help us figure out who we can be. (30)

And now, a few years later, I would add to this that our stories' and others' stories' interdependence means that sharing a story of misogyny in the academic workplace makes it possible for others to share more stories of misogyny in the academic workplace. Stories create possibility. They tell us *what happened* but they also allow us to understand differently, in different terms and with different means of selection and evaluation (Frank, *Letting* 46) what is real, what is possible, what is "worth doing or best avoided" (Frank, *Letting* 3).

The more stories told about misogyny in English departments, the less precarious each individual story becomes. From individual, isolated stories, we build a collective, and that collective becomes a rich site of narrative resources from which future storytellers can draw. Though each individual woman I spoke with told her stories only to me, she knew I was talking with others, and she knew that her story would join together with the stories of other women to form a collective, a collective that would accomplish significant social and rhetorical work that her story alone could not do. And it is this social and rhetorical work that, I argue, persuaded many of the women to push past the self-monitoring to tell their stories.

In the rest of this Introduction, I draw on women's responses to the final question of my interviews[2]—What made you want to want to be part of this project and share your stories?—to identify the kinds of precariousness women's stories of misogyny are subjected to. I begin with Arthur Frank's concept of *narrative habitus* as a way to bolster the concept of precarious narratives by arguing that the stories that are not part of our narrative habitus are more precarious and need more social support. I show how this narrative habitus that we all possess

---

2 In analyzing the data for this Introduction, I separated out the responses to this final question and examined them separately from the rest of the interview data to determine what, if any, patterns emerged. I then categorized them based on codes such as *gossip, job guilt, retaliation,* and *storytelling.*

to some degree or another persuaded women in my interview project to share their experiences with me in order to contribute to a collective of stories. This collective challenges patriarchy's demand that women care for men's needs and shifts the focus to women's needs instead. It is thus likely to be subject to more misogyny. I believe that many of the women I spoke with understood this from the start. I point then to three anticipated punishments interviewees articulated; my doing so demonstrates that our narrative habitus has developed with a tacit understanding of how misogyny functions. While the stories women told me are *about* punishment, their very telling was constrained by their tellers' anticipation of being punished for telling.

Storytelling about misogyny in a patriarchy is never as simple as just telling; the very telling itself is constrained by the norms of patriarchy. When these norms are challenged, misogyny awaits to shock women back into place.

Narrative Habitus and the Powers of Storytelling

In *Letting Stories Breathe: A Socio-Narratology*, Arthur W. Frank describes a narrative habitus as "a *repertoire* of stories that a person at least recognizes and that a group shares." I want to highlight two characteristics of narrative habitus here. First, Frank writes that narrative habitus "is the feel for what story makes a good follow-up to a previous story, what story fits which occasion; who wants to hear what story when. A person's narrative habitus enables knowing how to react when a story is told, according to what kind of story it is. Complementary to that competence, narrative habitus enables prediction of how others will react to a story that might be told" (53). Another way of saying this is that a person's narrative habitus encompasses her body of narrative resources and that those resources inform our understanding of how a story will perform rhetorically. Narrative habitus is about *anticipation*. A second characteristic of narrative habitus that is relevant to this work is that "narrative habitus predisposes a sense of the right and fitting resolution toward which a half-told story should progress; it is the feel for what kind of narrative move leads to what next kind of move" (54). Frank continues, "People's sense of how plots will probably go reflects and generates their everyday common sense of which actions lead to which consequences, whether in stories or in life. People's habitus of expected plot completions is nothing less than their sense of life's possibilities" (54). We know how so many stories will go. We have developed a finely tuned narrative habitus based on years of living in a patriarchy, so we know that when we begin to tell a story in which we have experienced some form of misogyny, we will be subject to some form of victim-blaming. We will be punished. We will be subject to further misogyny. Our stories, before we even share them, are precarious from the start.

But our narrative habitus tells us that there are powers to storytelling. We know, because we have experienced it before, how stories change us, how they shape and reshape our belief systems, how they function rhetorically to direct and redirect our attention. Of the social nature of storytelling, Frank writes,

> Stories connect people into collectivities, and they coordinate actions among people who share the expectation that life will unfold according to certain plots. The selves and collectivities animated by stories then animate further stories: revising old stories and creating new ones—though whether any story is every truly new is always contestable. Stories and humans work together, in symbiotic dependency, *creating the social* that comprises all human relationships, collectivities, mutual dependencies, and exclusions. (*Letting,* emphasis in original; 15)

Women knew they were involved in building a collective, one whose individual stories would be used to animate further stories, "revising old stories and creating new ones." They knew that the work they were doing was part of something larger that had the power to do what only stories can do.[3]

One of the powers of storytelling that participants pointed to was simply the sheer breaking of the silence that has surrounded misogyny in English departments until now. One participant told me, "It is so frustrating to be part of a program that I love that performs inclusivity and yet does not always live up to inclusivity and in some cases flat out rewards misogyny and racism and all of the other isms. It is exhausting. So anything we can try to do to shine light on these practices I think has got to be good and helpful. It will be painful but it needs to happen." Similarly, another participant said, "I think that the only way to stop this is to first acknowledge that it happens, so I feel like we have to share our stories and I feel like even one story, even if you don't think it's extreme, is important to share."

Related to the need to simply get the stories on record was the recognition that stories accomplish the important rhetorical work of letting others know that they are not alone. This message came up a number of times as a benefit of sharing stories of misogyny in the workplace. One woman noted, "I think it's

---

3 Twenty-two of thirty-nine women pointed to the powers of storytelling as the reason they wanted to share their stories with me and, by extension, you.

important to identify the sheer number of women who experience these issues and let other women know that they aren't alone so that they might feel inclined to step forward and tell their stories." This woman understands that one power of storytelling is that it begets further storytelling; one of the healing powers of knowing you're not alone is that you may feel safe enough to share your own story. Another woman said, "I feel like saying, you can be in these awful, awful departments, but just leaving sometimes is best. Often I find that misogyny is like a toxic, abusive relationship—they want to hold you there. I want other people to know they're not alone." Both of these women's recognition of the power of knowing you're not alone is echoed in this participant's words: "It's like, when you've gone through this stuff, you think, who can do anything else to me, and if my story makes someone else go, that's exactly what's happening to me, then that's great. Because we've got to get the stories out."

I have long understood that one of the most important effects of storytelling is that it makes readers and listeners feel less alone, but it had been a long time since I had stopped to think about just what was so awful about feeling alone. Having been caught up in hearing so many women's stories while working on this project, I had stopped feeling alone with my own experiences of misogyny, and I had momentarily forgotten how isolating my own experiences had felt for so long. Three women specifically shared with me their feelings of *just needing to share their stories with someone*—me—because they had felt so isolated during the experiences they described. One participant explained that her reasons for talking with me were multiple: "Part of it is because I know that I'm not the only person experiencing this stuff but the other part is that right now I don't have anyone I can tell, you know?" Another participant recognized that being part of this project means that *she* is not alone: "I guess also to be part of something that acknowledges that I'm not alone. I think what's scariest about this is how isolated it made me feel." A third woman told me this:

> I've wanted to tell people about this experience just because I felt so isolated and alone walking through this by myself. I just needed to tell somebody what happened. And I think sometimes people think, well, you're just being too sensitive. The scope and gravity of it, at the end of the day, the scope and gravity of what can happen to people because of it, I just needed somebody to know. I will say, though, that I almost canceled fourteen times. I've been sweating this. I'm supposed to be able to handle this. Other people—it didn't seem to upset them that I was going through this, so I should just be able to accept this. It makes me weak because I can't.

Looking around your own department and seeing that others are not affected by the pain you are feeling, that others are not affected by misogyny in the same ways you are can be incredibly isolating, and we all know that a sense of belonging is a crucial human need. One can hear, too, in this participant's words, the internalized shaming as she characterizes herself as someone who *should* be able to handle the misogyny her department subjected her to once she became chair.

Related to participants' desire for others to know they are not alone is their desire to help others avoid the kind of misogyny they've had to experience. One participant said, "I want to participate to show that it's not just sexual harassment.... I wanted to talk about how a lot of the messages I've gotten have been couched in protection: 'I care about you as a colleague, so I'm encouraging you to do this rather than that.'... In my experience of reading accounts like this, if I had been a graduate student and read an article like this, I think it would have been nice." Another participant put her desire more directly: "There are moments when I look back at my history where something I have said has triggered an actual action and a change in somebody's life for the better and that is what I am trying to do here." Similarly, a third participant told me, "I also really, really want to believe that if you talk it can help people.... I want to believe that talking can help and I'm tired of it having to be me whispering to my undergrads, don't take this professor, he treats women differently. I want it to be something more legitimate. I hope that this can help. I hope the right people read it and take it to heart."

Finally, one woman's reasons for participating in this project pointed to the effects of our *not* sharing our stories with each other and with students:

> It's something that we have to be aware of and I do think that women in departments are constantly—at least I and my colleagues are—wanting to be supportive of students but at the same time, especially with female students, we want them to have a tough skin and the people who come to English departments are the people who are often looking for ways to talk about things that have happened to them. They want to do it in a way that captures their emotions, they want to be angry, they want to learn to express things, but they are constantly worried about the perception and evaluation of that work. We have a lot of creative writers and a lot of the involved students on our campus are that way—they feel inclined to write confessionally but they also don't want to be considered reactionary and finding that balance is so hard for them especially. They're twenty years old.

Our conversation continued, and we talked about her point that so many students come to English departments because they want to tell their stories, and it often becomes clear to them that we aren't telling *our* stories. Our asking students to write their stories but refusing to share our stories sends the message that we believe in the power of storytelling for them but not for us. As another participant said, "The graduate students can't talk about it because they're in such a terribly vulnerable position and they know if we aren't talking about it, that we're hiding something because they're experiencing it and they don't know why we're hiding it." Perhaps they do know why we're hiding it; indeed, my data suggests that many graduate students are well aware of the ways patriarchy works to push all women down.

Additional Social Supports

In addition to the powers of storytelling, interviewees pointed to two other reasons for their willingness to share their stories with me. Recall that all narratives are precarious, that they require support from the social and cultural world, and that the more social and cultural support they receive, the less precarious they become. Participants pointed to two kinds of social support they felt for their storytelling: their own positioning as women who were in a safe space in their academic careers and a feeling of trust in me, their interviewer.

First, participants pointed to their own positions as women who were no longer precarious in terms of age or status in the university.[4] One doctoral student told me that she felt comfortable sharing her story with me because "I'm in a very good place in my life where I'm able to reflect on this. I'm in a loving and supportive program. I'm not necessarily sure I would have come forward in my negative Master's program experience." Similarly, another participant pointed to her sense that she was in a good place: "I was thinking, for the most part, I have it okay. I've heard horror stories and the fact that I have an amazing department chair who lets me do the work I want to do and who helps me feel valued and the fact that she's a woman helps with that. I know I could have it a lot worse. I'll just put it that way." One can hear, in this participant's characterization of her chair as letting her do the work she wants to do, an understanding not only that that is not always the case in other programs, but also that women in academia do not have the default ability to do the work we want to do.

---

4 Eight of thirty-nine women pointed to their own status or place in the university as a reason for being willing to speak with me.

For other women, there was the sense that it took years to develop the kind of temerity that is required to be able to tell the stories they shared with me. "I'm at a point in my life that I think I have garnered enough strength and authority that I have a responsibility to be more vocal because I'm recognizing that I'm safer than I've ever been, particularly having just been promoted to full professor so if full professors can't talk then, my god, who can?" one woman told me. Similarly, another participant shared with me that part of her reason for talking with me was job security:

> Part of it is that I'm tenured and I have separated myself emotionally from the institution enough because the institution is so messed up that I do my work, I work hard, but I'm not working for [the institution]. I'm working for the students and I'm working as a researcher but I'm trying to keep my distance from other things. Partly it's my power and partly I've been talking with people about this, especially at [my institution], with graduate students, for thirteen years now and I don't see that it's getting much better.

And then there was the woman who pointed to both job security and age when she told me, "I'm tenured and I'm over forty. And I'm done.… You've got to be a certain sort of pissed off and a certain sort of secure.… In graduate school, I probably would've been like, what are these women complaining about, and now I'm like, I have many complaints! Listen to my complaints!" Age factors importantly in one's willingness to speak about mistreatment; the older one gets, it seems, the less willing one is to accept misogyny as simply part of how academia works. Finally, the length of time one has been experiencing misogyny in one's department figures importantly in these women's decisions to tell their stories; while one woman has been talking with others at her institution about these issues for thirteen years, another is just "done." As another participant said to me, "Silence equals death. Sometimes we may not feel like we can talk and sometimes we can't but when we get strong enough.… It's not gonna get better if we're quiet. We're just gonna die quietly."

Second, many women I spoke with trusted their audience. About a quarter of the women I spoke with were people I knew personally or professionally, and it turns out that my ethos or my reputation in the field was one of the reasons some of the participants felt comfortable sharing their stories with me.[5] As one woman

---

5 Seven of thirty-nine women named knowing me or knowing of my work as a reason for feeling comfortable talking with me.

put it, she understood me as an outlet where "you're not gonna be seen as someone who's complaining. You're not gonna be seen as someone who instigated it or that it's your fault. Even though that's the way we're made to feel. I was definitely made to feel like I had acted inappropriately and this was my punishment for it."

One participant told me she felt a "duty of care" to participate in the project because she had always had positive interactions with me. Another said that I seemed like "a real person, someone who is safe," and that sentiment is echoed in how others characterized the ways they believed I would treat their data. "I'll say on a personal level, I know you and I know you're a good, qualified researcher and I trust that you would be responsible with my data and that kind of thing, so that of course makes me feel less worried about something getting out." Another participant told me that she decided to participate because "I've known you so long and I know the honesty with which you'll handle the project, so it's wanting to participate in a project with someone whose scholarship I admire and value." Another woman noted that she believed that "What I had to say would be used effectively and that I didn't feel in danger. I have to say, if I just saw this from somebody that I didn't know, I may not have done it because I would be scared that it wouldn't be confidential or that they might identify me and I could get in trouble." We hear the threat in these statements, the idea that a different researcher might not treat their words confidentially and they might, thus, be subjected to misogynistic punishment for having shared their stories.

Anticipated Punishments

Manne points to a number of what she calls down-girl moves that often follow a woman breaking the norms of obligation and entitlement; she writes:

> Girls and women may be down-ranked or deprived relative to more or less anything that people typically value—material goods, social status, moral reputation, and intellectual credentials, among other realms of human achievement, esteem, pride, and so on. This may happen in numerous ways: condescending, mansplaining, moralizing, blaming, punishing, silencing, lampooning, satirizing, sexualizing, belittling, caricaturizing, exploiting, erasing, and evincing pointed indifference.

Any one of these moves acts as a shock collar, shocking a woman back into place when she has strayed beyond her station. For the women I spoke with, a narrative habitus that suggests how others will respond to their stories of misogyny in English departments led to their identifying three anticipated punishments that they nevertheless risked in order to share their experiences with me. I outline these anticipated punishments in this section to emphasize the bravery and strength of the women I spoke with, and also to reinforce that telling stories is not the simple sharing of experiences. It requires forethought and risk, a savvy narrative habitus, and an understanding that sharing stories toward greater awareness is only the first step toward change.

The first of these anticipated punishments is being labeled a gossip.[6] Recall what Micciche writes in *Composition Studies'* Where We Are Section: that gossip serves as a kind of protection among colleagues. She writes, "We've heard stories passed discreetly among friends at conferences and in hallways" (11). One interview participant told me, toward the end of our conversation, "I am concerned because as women we're told our whole lives that what we do is gossip and I am a tattler. I still am a tattler. That's a way of self-protection that the patriarchy is always trying to steal from us." That nobody wants to be understood as a gossip is evident from the many sayings we have about those who gossip: snitches get stitches; you never look good trying to make someone else look bad; if you don't have anything nice to say, don't say anything at all. What all of these sayings share in common is the belief that it's the words themselves, rather than the actions they are describing, that are the problem when one person tells another about a third person's wrongdoing. Characterizing testimony about misogyny as gossip minimizes that testimony in ways that harm the speaker because she is understood to possess little self-control. In addition, the person who is the subject of the so-called gossip becomes the victim of gossip as a kind of aggression, the result often being that sympathy may flow directly to the perpetrators of misogyny rather than to the victims in an example of what Manne has coined "himpathy."

Women are disciplined very early to believe that what they are doing when they complain is not legitimate but rather gossiping or tattling. As one participant put it, "A lot of times self-regulation is something that women learn. It's very insert-Foucault stage left. We learn it and then we monitor ourselves." As a result, there's a kind of pre-screening we go through even before we get to the point of complaint, a pre-screening that finds us editing out what we consider to be less egregious instances of misogyny. As another participant put it, "When I thought

---

6 Six of thirty-nine women pointed to being labeled a gossip as a means of feeling silenced.

about, do I have any experiences, they all sounded really small, so I also felt like my experiences weren't big enough or extreme enough to warrant being named misogynistic, but I also know better than that and when I started making my list and I thought about the totality of what those experiences looked like, I realized they were pretty big." Another interviewee noted, when relaying a story about a specific person in her department, "This is where I feel like I'm just airing grievances," a strong indication that she is accustomed to monitoring what she says for their likelihood of making her out to be a gossip.

Women recognize what happens to their words when they are characterized as "just gossips," as evidenced by this interview participant, who said,

> I appreciated being able to have the platform to tell the story, but I also want to think more about what it means for us to be told that we can't—that we'll be seen as just gossips or—I think the word that keeps coming up is retaliation and so I think in academia just like in lots of fields and businesses there's this expectation that you'll maintain this façade that everything is fine, that no one's racist, that no one's sexist, or any of those things.

This woman understands that being labeled a gossip has a rhetorical function, and that that function is to dismiss our testimony. Gossip, as James C. Scott notes, "almost by definition, has no identifiable author," and its goal is typically "to ruin the reputation of some identifiable person or persons" (142). When women who testify to misogyny understand that they are at risk of being dismissed as mere gossips, they understand that they are seen as aiming to ruin individual men's reputations rather than testifying to a systemic problem. They also understand that their own reputations are at stake, and it is here that we can see being characterized as a gossip as a down-girl move. Women know they are risking being down-ranked in terms of social status and moral reputation when they speak out about abuse.

But—need it be said?—women who testify to misogyny in their workplaces are not gossips. They are not tattletales. One woman told me that the very existence of this study gave her hope; she said, "I really appreciate that you're doing this work....Just reading the description of your study made me feel validated, even if I never talked to you because I thought, this is a real thing. I'm not floundering in this void. Other people see that this is happening. So that was very important." *Other people see that this is happening.* When we are made to believe that we are just gossips, we are also made to believe that what we are saying is not true, that it is not being witnessed by others. Being labeled a gossip is a form of gaslighting.

A second anticipated punishment identified by interviewees is being perceived as ungrateful for their hard-won jobs in a difficult academic job market.[7] This is particularly difficult because, as Manne suggests, women are obligated to deliver feminine-coded goods such as gratitude and *not* to seem entitled to masculine-coded perks like security and respect. At a time when the value of the Humanities, generally, and English studies specifically, is questioned regularly both inside and outside of academia, the silencing of women can be expected to proceed apace. As one interviewee put it to me,

> To basically say, "This is how it is," even at a moment when we're supposed to say, "Oh don't say anything bad about English departments because they'll cut us," is exactly the kind of move that's important because there are a lot of people all over the country who are working in these situations and who think they have to be—they have to not stand up because they may lose their job or they think they have to not stand up because their college will be closed otherwise, so I think there's also this way in which, particularly in times of tight budgets, we've been pressed not to complain or not identify the things that actually keep us from being successful in our jobs.

I responded to her by saying, "Of all times, this would be a time when you would stay silent, when the humanities are in crisis, and so just sort of put your head down, do your work, hope that we can get the majors up and just continue to accept the misogynistic treatment and be happy you have a job." Her response to me:

> Be happy you have a job. I think this goes back to perpetrating these kinds of systems further into the future. That's what you're modeling for students: we don't stand up for things because we want to protect our jobs. We're in some way also raising generations of students who kind of think pretending nothing's happening is the way to go. It's almost like counter the mission of the humanities. You want to raise critical thinkers, but you just say, "Oh, don't think about this. Don't think about that. Think about that little thing that's important here."

---

7   Three of thirty-nine women anticipated being perceived as ungrateful for their jobs as a means of being silenced.

There is so much to appreciate in this participant's commentary on what it means to speak the truth in a time when doing so might be interpreted by others as ingratitude for the jobs we hold; I'll point here to two significant points. First, I think her point about now being the exact time to point to the problems with misogyny because the climate surrounding the humanities for so long has been austere suggests that some of those who were willing to talk with me were willing to push past the narrative that to be grateful for one's job is also to grin and bear misogyny in the workplace. Second, there is perhaps no phrase more ubiquitous in the humanities than critical thinking, but we do not often stop and articulate the appropriate objects of that critical thought; this interviewee's point about our raising students to think about this little thing over here, but not *this*, not these crucially significant issues affecting us in the workplace, draws attention to the limits of our alleged critical thinking pedagogies.

Another participant who described harrowing experiences in her department said, "I don't think people realize that getting a tenure-track position in the humanities is like winning the lottery.... I have to remember that for some people this would be a gift." Even as she has just finished telling me about experiences that were scary and isolating, this participant told me, "I feel a lot of guilt for being dissatisfied. I try to talk myself out of feeling badly because other people would want [this job]." One can almost hear her reconciling the warring parts of her mind as she talks to me. She wants to tell me about her experiences; she doesn't want to be seen as ungrateful, so she tries to talk herself out of feeling bad. This is one effect of the powerful narrative of a tight humanities job market; our narrative habitus helps us predict how the story will go.

Finally, the punishment anticipated by more women than any other[8], the end that our narrative habitus fills in for us when we imagine telling our stories of misogyny in our academic workplaces, is retaliation[9].

Two doctoral students point indirectly to the possibility of retaliation, one when she says, "With two Title IX cases in the past year and a half, there's not really a lot I can say that's going to hurt me because I've said so many things," and

---

8 Eight of thirty-nine women mentioned a fear of retaliation for sharing their stories with me.

9 We also see this fear of retaliation in the silences of *Presumed Incompetent*. As Harris and Gonzalez write, "a significant number of women decided not to contribute to the anthology for fear of retaliation. They believed they would be penalized for airing their home institution's dirty laundry in public, and they were not prepared to become pariahs" (11).

the other when she reflects on the possibility of not being able to have a career in the field. She says, "There's also sort of being in this position where I no longer care that, like, it sounds horrible, if for some reason, I couldn't have this career anymore, I would just move on because it's been horrible anyway, and I would just find a way to carry on with my life." Both students recognize that there is the possibility for others to hurt them, to damage their reputations or careers, but at the same time, both mitigate that understanding by contrasting it with either past or future scenarios in which they have or will survive academia.

Told from the start that all names and identifying information would be kept confidential as part of the research process, participants took comfort in the protection of anonymity. The discourse of retaliation is strong in this participant's response: "This is anonymous too so it's not like it's going to affect me and I found out about it through my department, so I don't feel like if they found out I participated there would be repercussions. I'm probably never going to apply for another leadership position after three times being shot down, at least not until I do some other stuff first, so I'm happy with my position. I like the job I have. I don't feel like there will be repercussions for me doing this." One gets the sense that this participant anticipates being found out, being *caught*, and having the protection of having learned about the project via someone in the department. Learning of the project via a department listserv is much less illicit, in other words, than learning of the project via social media. The listserv seems to sanction the project and sanction the storytelling.

Another participant interprets the anonymity of the project a bit differently. She says, "The maddening thing here is that there's not anything any of us can actually do about it. I'm not even using his name here. And if I did, with the gender dynamic, the reality is that I'm the one who would be on the hot seat for being such a bitch to call so-and-so out." As we saw above, another participant makes a similar point when she notes that "we'll be seen as gossips or—I think the word that keeps coming up is retaliation" for naming a particular person at a particular place who is engaging in misogynistic behaviors. Recall that she said, "I think in academia just like in lots of fields and businesses there's this expectation that you'll maintain this façade that everything is fine, that no one's racist, that no one's sexist, or any of those things." Maintaining that façade functions as a kind of protection against retaliation.

Sara Ahmed writes that "we are often encouraged to think of our careers as having an exteriority, as *what* you have to care for in order to have somewhere to go," and the same participant who pointed to the need for a façade that "everything is fine," told me that she knew if she talked with anybody outside her department about what was happening, she risked the stability of that career.

> If I were to tell anyone outside my department, would that negatively impact my getting tenure if I stayed, would it negatively impact my ability to move up at this school? It just always felt like I was stepping out on that ledge, and I was going to hurt myself. I think I've been wondering more what it is we're really protecting by doing that. I think by the time I left the last place, I had thought, do I care enough about being in this field and doing this very specific job that I would stay in a place where this was happening? Would I rather just leave if I can't find a job somewhere else? I think that's one of the consequences—how many women leave instead of dealing with it.

The potential for retaliation in the form of down-girl moves such as silencing, punishing, deprivation of advancement, diminished career prospects—all of these were understood in advance by many of the women I interviewed. All of these function for so many women—those who have stories but who chose not to talk with me—as prolepsis; they are, in Leigh Gilmore's words, "a threat that prevents women from testifying" (7). They are the ending we anticipate.[10]

Because here's the thing. Whether we want to admit it or not, there are some of us in English departments with more power than others. There are some of us who wield that power in ways we would rather not have pointed out to us. We do not like to have our own bad behavior called out. But we all accede to patriarchal norms and we all engage in behaviors that function to punish women who stray from those norms, even as we stand at the front of our classrooms and talk about the vagaries of power. There are so few people writing or talking about the abuses we experience in our workplaces; it's time that silencing stops. Sady Doyle writes,

---

10 One might wonder why, if participants knew ahead of time that their names would be kept confidential, they would be worried about retaliation. This is a rational question. Retaliation is not a rational fear. What I mean by this is that we have been conditioned by patriarchy to believe that if we violate a patriarchal norm, we will be punished. Though names are not attached to the stories women told in this case, such ingrained fear is not so easily assuaged. I am here to tell you that women were afraid of retaliation and I think that this suggests that patriarchy remains remarkably successful in keeping that fear alive in women despite assurances from a researcher. That women went ahead and told their stories is testament to their selflessness and care for other women.

Women incur a risk every time they shift from passive to active voice; from *women are oppressed* to *you are oppressing me*. One is acknowledged fact. One's fighting words. The second statement requires that a man see himself as a person in power. It requires him to admit that, "leftist" politics or no, he is not the hero in every story. (90)

To Doyle's insight, I would only add that such active voice also requires that *she* admit that she is not the hero in every story. For not all those who engage in misogynist behavior are men. Many are women who have risen to power by following very closely the rules of patriarchy.

Overview of Chapters

Despite the risks of punishment, thirty-nine women shared stories with me. In Chapter 1, "Silencing Women's Voices in Academic Spaces," I share women's experiences of having their voices erased and effaced on a regular basis in committee and department meetings, in the case of faculty, and in classrooms, in the case of graduate students. I introduce the concept of "hepeating," which happens when a man repeats a woman's comment verbatim and is heard in ways she had not been. The result of so much silencing is that women begin to self-silence, no longer trying to participate in academic exchange.

Chapter 2, "The Expectation to Serve and Care for Others," shares stories women told me about men getting away with doing less service and women being expected to do more. The women I spoke with felt pressure to take on more service than they could do at the same time that they saw the men around them getting out of service commitments or performing service so poorly that nobody wanted them to do it for fear they would just create more problems. I also consider the difficulty so many women have saying "No," and the ways we are socialized to take on more work than our male colleagues.

In Chapter 3, "Masculine-Coded Goods in English Departments: Respect, Authority, Leadership," I share stories women told me about asking for and being refused masculine-coded goods such as respect, authority, and salary, and I identify the punishments they endured for having asked for such goods. In these stories, we see women asking for goods that are, in a patriarchy, understood to be his alone for the taking: "leadership, authority, influence, money, and other forms of power, as well as social status, prestige, rank, and the markers thereof" (Manne, *Down Girl* 113). Sometimes women just take them, rather than asking for them, and often, women are punished by being shocked back into place: being given more work to do, not getting the promotion, being questioned about their capabilities, being characterized as aggressive or too assertive.

Chapter 4, "Sexual Harassment and Women's Credibility," focuses on stories of sexual harassment in English departments, both witnessed and experienced. The goal of this chapter is to disabuse us of the belief that we are somehow above the fray when it comes to sexual harassment.

Chapter 5, "On Gaslighting," shares stories of individual gaslighting in English departments, and it identifies two forms of leverage used by those in English departments to get away with the gaslighting. The first form of leverage stems from the deeply held belief that women cannot be misogynists, so when women experience misogyny from other women, they second-guess their experiences. And the second form of leverage stems from the pervasive belief that English departments are committed to social justice, diversity, and inclusivity. When women experience misogyny in departments whose commitments to these values are explicit, they lend more credence to the departments' vision and second-guess their own experiences.

Chapter 6 is named for the biggest effect of all of this misogyny: "Women No Longer Want to Give." In this chapter, I examine stories about the effects of this misogyny on women's personal and work lives. Misogyny leads to damaged health in the form of anxiety, stress, depression, and exhaustion, and it leads women to disengage in the work of their departments. This chapter details the effects on women's productivity, and it includes the stories of women who left their jobs—and, in two cases, the academy altogether—in large part because of misogyny.

Finally, in the last chapter, "Less Precarious Stories," I consider what it will take for these stories to be heard, and what English departments might do differently to combat the misogyny that women experience every day.

This work aims to break the silence surrounding misogyny in English departments in the United States. I am not so naïve as to believe that doing so will automatically alter our working conditions. But because we are the keepers of narrative, the scholars who lay claim to understanding how narratives work, how they travel, how they effect change, perhaps when we recognize the ways we are, ourselves, living the same old tired misogynistic narratives, we might think twice. In her memoir, *Notes on a Silencing* about her experience of abuse at the prestigious St. Paul's School in New Hampshire, Lacy Crawford writes,

> The work of telling is essential, and it is not enough. There is always the danger that the energy of the injustice will exhaust itself in the revelation—that we will be horrified but remain unchanged. The reason for this, I suspect, is that these are stories we already know. *A girl was assaulted. A boy was molested.* The producer, the judge, the bishop, the boss. To hear these stories spoken aloud is jarring, but not because it causes us to reconsider who we are and how we are organized. It is only when power is threatened that power responds. (379)

Very likely none of the stories you are about to read are new to you. Perhaps this makes them matter more. They are a part of our narrative habitus; we know what happens when those with more power interact with those with less power, when those with less power do not cleave to the wishes of those with more. And if they *are* new to you, well, it's time to wake up, to look around, to recognize that we in English departments are not immune to the forces of patriarchy. Your female colleagues are not human givers. They are human beings and deserve respect.

I conducted this research and I wrote this book before the fall of Roe v. Wade in June, 2022, but the deep misogyny structuring that decision clearly makes this work more relevant than even I had imagined when I first set out to do it. Women's rights are under attack in this country, and if we are going to claim that the academy is a safe space for women, that we teach diversity, inclusion, and equity, we must take a good hard look at what we're doing to one another first. That can only begin if we listen honestly to women's stories of misogyny in the academic workplace.

References

Ahmed, Sara. "Warnings." *Feminist Killjoys*, 3 Dec. 2018.

Crawford, Lacy. *Notes on a Silencing*. New York: Little, Brown and Company, 2020.

Doyle, Sady. "Nowhere Left to Go." *Believe Me*. Ed. Jessica Valenti and Jaclyn Friedman. New York: Seal Press, 2020. 83–92.

Elder, Cristyn L., and Bethany Davila, Ed. *Defining, Locating, and Addressing Bullying in the WPA Workplace*. Logan: Utah State UP, 2019.

Ericsson, Patricia Freitag, Ed. *Sexual Harassment and Cultural Change in Writing Studies*. Fort Collins, CO: The WAC Clearinghouse, 2020.

Frank, Arthur W. *Letting Stories Breathe: A Socio-Narratology*. Chicago: The University of Chicago Press, 2010.

———. "Tricksters and Truth Tellers: Narrating Illness in an Age of Authenticity and Appropriation." *Literature and Medicine* 28.2 (2009): 185–199.

Gilmore, Leigh. *Tainted Witness: Why We Doubt What Women Say About Their Lives*. New York: Columbia UP, 2017.

Graeber, David. "The Bully's Pulpit: On the Elementary Structure of Domination." *The Baffler* 28 (July 2015).

Lusher, Katelyn. "Academic Spaces and Grad Student Harassment." *Composition Studies* 46.2 (2018): 198–199.

Manne, Kate. *Down Girl: The Logic of Misogyny*. New York: Oxford UP, 2018.

Micciche, Laura. "From the Editor." *Composition Studies* 46.2 (2018): 10–11.

Penaluna, Regan. "Kate Manne: The Shock Collar That Is Misogyny." *Guernica*, 7 Feb. 2018.

Robillard, Amy E. *We Find Ourselves in Other People's Stories: On Narrative Collapse and a Lifetime Search for Story*. New York: Routledge, 2019.

Scott, James C. *Domination and the Arts of Resistance: Hidden Transcripts*. New Haven: Yale UP, 1990.

Sicari, Anna. "Centering the Conversation: Patriarchy, Academic Culture, and #MeToo." *Composition Studies* 46.2 (2018): 200–202.

Solnit, Rebecca. "A Short History of Silence." *The Mother of All Questions*. Chicago: Haymarket, 2017. 17–66.

Twale, Darla J. *Understanding and Preventing Faculty-on-Faculty Bullying*. New York: Routledge, 2017.

Twale, Darla J., and Barbara M. De Luca, Ed. *Faculty Incivility: The Rise of the Academic Bully Culture and What to Do About It*. San Francisco: Jossey-Bass, 2008.

1

Silencing Women's Voices in Academic Spaces

"When a woman tells the truth," the poet Adrienne Rich wrote, "she is creating the possibility for more truth around her." I am telling you that silence and disbelief work that way, too, in concentric circles, radiating out from the people or topics you intend to shut down. The radius of that silence travels farther and faster than you'd think.

—Sady Doyle, "Nowhere Left to Go"

A trans woman friend of mine recently explained to me how the technique for training your voice to sound more feminine has a lot to do "with speaking less or asking more questions or deferring to other people more."

—Melissa Febos, "Thank You for Taking Care of Yourself"

Molly, an assistant professor and Writing Program Administrator (WPA) at a Hispanic-serving institution, tells me a story that involved a man's attempts to silence her, to belittle her, and to intimidate her, all in a meeting with their department chair. As a new WPA, Molly had been in charge of creating new policies that this man, whom Molly never names but I'll call George for the sake of storytelling, had never had to abide by when he had taught for the university years earlier. George had been away from the institution for some years, as it had been discovered that he didn't actually have the proper credentials to be teaching the courses he'd been put in charge of. After accruing enough credits in a Master's in composition program, George would be returning to the campus to teach introductory composition courses, specifically ENG 096, which is the university's foundational course populated by what Molly calls "our most fragile group of students." The things that Molly heard about him before she met him were that "he was extraordinarily well liked by students" and that he had "refused to teach the 096 courses because, by his wording, the students were too stupid to be in college, they didn't belong, he didn't connect with them the way he connected with all his other students." When Molly met with George for the first time, he assured her that he was able and enthusiastic about teaching ENG 096. During that meeting, George showered her with what Molly characterized as "weird self-deprecating flattery" by saying things like, "You know, I'm just an old man, I'm not as smart as you." She did not respond to that language, and kept the focus instead on his teaching for the program.

Before the start of the next semester, Molly organized a meeting for all instructors to go over the new assessment plan, and during that meeting she noticed that "his face was very red and he was staring at the floor. He would not make eye contact with me." When she got to the part of the meeting about ENG 096's assessment plan, George looked up at her for the first time and, "with his face really red, says, 'How do you expect me to teach research? They can barely write a sentence.'" Molly responds calmly that they are, indeed, capable of conducting research, and George says,

> "They can barely write their own names. I don't know how you expect me to get them to understand MLA citation," and he started getting really loud, very agitated. And he stands up, and I just sort of like backed up to the smart board and just folded my arms and I'm thinking, I don't know if this guy's going to attack me or what, I have no idea. The other women in the room—this is an interesting part—started comforting him and sort of saying, "Oh, it's okay, we know you haven't been here in a while." They had this tone in their voice of sort of, this poor old man. Meanwhile, I'm just standing there looking at him like, you're dangerous to me at this point.

Immediately after this meeting, Molly informs her chair about George's behavior, and her chair sets up a mediation meeting among the three of them. About this meeting, Molly tells me, "Clearly something needs to be done, and if that's what it needs to be, then I will sacrifice my own dignity to make sure that this man is kept away from students." In the days leading up to the mediation meeting, Molly says, "I started thinking to myself, what course of action will I take here? Either I'm going to unload on him all of these things that I've heard and all of these things that I've observed and my fears of him interacting with students or I'm gonna sit back and let him be his own undoing. About three minutes into the mediation, I knew which course of action to take, and that was to sit back and let him be his own undoing."

At the meeting, their chair allows Molly to begin, and she does so by describing her concern for students, saying, among other things, "The opinions you expressed about them go against every instinct in my body about what education is." When she finishes, George sits back in his chair and, after being quiet for a few seconds, says, "you just speak such good Ph.D., don't you?" Though their chair interjects and says, "All right, we don't need to have that kind of tone," George continues.

> He points his finger at me—and he's a very large man—we're sitting across the table from one another, but he got pretty close to my face, and he said, "*She* is going to make this about how much I care about students. *She* is going to tell me that I don't know how to interact with students and that's bullshit," and so then I just decided in that moment, I'm just gonna sit here and I'm gonna let my department chair speak on my behalf because I'm not expending any more energy in this moment. This meeting went on for about another forty minutes. The general theme of this meeting, was him saying over and over to Steve that he could not work in this department as long as *she* is in charge. I cannot work here as long as *she* is telling me what to do. *She* is creating an environment in this department that is not helpful or productive. It was just over and over this *she she she she* with his finger pointing toward me.

With the help of her chair after this meeting, Molly filed a Title 5 complaint against George and, though the Title 5 investigation did not find gender-based discrimination despite the *she she she she* and the physical intimidation during the meeting, the Title 5 representative did make the recommendation that George be let go.

Molly was in a position of authority in the department, in a role that required that she issue instructions to others, and George could not accept instructions from a woman. That much is clear. In that meeting, George demonstrated an unwillingness to hear what Molly had to say, a sense that his words mattered more than hers, and a belief—though ultimately unfounded—that he could get away with treating her misogynistically in front of their chair. Molly tells me that her story "is something that I would imagine is not uncommon, that a male colleague unleashes on someone. I think what is uncommon about that story is that he was fired, that he was seen for the abuse that he was doling out and he was let go." This is not the way this kind of story usually ends. More frequently, a faculty member like George is slapped on the wrist and sent back to the classroom and someone like Molly is left to continue dealing with him. We know this. So Molly's story has something of a triumphant ending.

Many women in English departments do not experience this type of ending; rather, they experience, on a regular basis, the erasure and effacement of their voices in committee meetings and department meetings where nobody stomps out angrily but instead, colleagues carry on as usual. Because it is usual. In this chapter, I canvass the ways women's voices are erased and effaced in classrooms, in the case of graduate students, and in meeting rooms, in the case of faculty. What I've learned from talking with the women in my study is that the more frequently women are silenced in classrooms and meeting rooms, the more likely they are to silence themselves in classrooms and meeting rooms.

Hepeating: Repeating with a Difference

In her essay, "The Public Voice of Women," Mary Beard points to a situation she is sure most women anywhere in Great Britain, if not the world, have regularly discussed,

> whether in the office, or a committee room, council chamber, seminar or the House of Commons. How do I get my point heard? How do I get it noticed? How do I get to belong in the discussion? I'm sure it's something some men feel too but if there's one thing that we know bonds women of all backgrounds, of all political colours, in all kinds of business and profession, it's the classic experience of the failed intervention; you're at a meeting, you make a point, then a short silence follows, and after a few awkward seconds some man picks up where you had just left off: "What I was saying was…." You might as well never have opened your mouth, and you end up blaming both yourself and the men whose exclusive club the discussion appears to be.

Beard's point is of course an important one, as she is surely correct that women everywhere have had this experience of being dismissed in workplace meetings. But she points, earlier in her piece, to the famous *Punch* cartoon featuring Miss Triggs in which one of many men at the conference table says to Miss Triggs, "That's an excellent suggestion, Miss Triggs. Perhaps one of the men here would like to make it." And it is a consideration of this move, what one of my interviewees called *hepeating*, that I want to begin this chapter with. Hepeating might be understood as repeating with a difference. Hepeating happens when a woman says something in a meeting, gets no response, only to have a man repeat the very same thing she just said, gaining the traction her initial vocalization never got.

The woman who introduced the term to me I'll call Meg. Meg, a non-tenure-track instructor at a large R-1 university, told me about an instance of hepeating that was so obvious, she couldn't ignore it.

> I've had people tell me that it's called "hepeating." In a meeting where I would say, like, "What about pasta?" This was a meeting where it was just me and one other

male senior colleague and I literally said something as specific as, "Well, what about pasta with red sauce and pink forks?" and he was like, "But what about pasta with red sauce and pink forks?" and it was really surreal because it was so exact and strange.... It was like it didn't even register that he had done it. It was about a grant proposal.

Recall that Manne theorizes misogyny as the enforcement of patriarchal norms, those norms being that men are entitled to *take* masculine-coded goods such as respect, authority, influence, and competitive advantage—and women are obligated to *give* feminine-coded goods such as attention, affection, care, adoration, indulgence, empathy, and loyalty. When we consider *attention* as a social good that women are expected to give to men and we take into account the patriarchal norm that men are entitled to *authority*, we can see that the way this is likely to play itself out in academic meetings is that women are expected to be listeners while the men speak. Further, we can conceptualize *credit* for ideas in academic meetings as a social good that the patriarchy would grant men but not women, making a phenomenon like hepeating a typical occurrence. When a man repeats the very thing a woman has just said and nobody bats an eye, everybody in the room is adhering to the norms that tell us that men deserve credit for ideas and women do not.

We can see this clearly in an exchange I had with an interviewee I'll call Gwen, an associate professor at a large public university. She tells me that she understands men in department meetings to have the attitude of

> 'I want to talk. I should be able to talk right now. And I would like to say all of these things and I should be able to talk ad nauseam, ad infinitum—and about anything that might even be tangentially related because I would like to. And if I so desire to stop speaking, it is because I decided to and for that you should be grateful.' That's what I feel like the experience is. It's not always so bombastically proclaimed, but that's the energy of it, so that's the expectation.

Gwen continues, pointing to a habit she sees in women, one that is consistent with the norms Manne identifies.

> I feel like a lot of the women have been socialized to defer and so—for example, the different experiences I have had in meetings where it's just women and it's like, "Oh, I'm sorry, I interrupted you." "Oh no, that's okay, go ahead." "Oh, okay, well, this." And also, naming the other person's contribution. My experience is that men will take your contribution, put their name on it, act like they came up with it, and want to take credit for it. They'll take your contribution and

take credit for it. Whereas what I experience with the women is often naming the contribution of the other woman or the man. "Oh well, Sally said this, blah blah blah…I'm gonna piggyback on this thing that Monica said." And that way you can see the trail of the idea.

I tell Gwen that, during the course of my interviews, I learned that this is called hepeating.

> Hepeating. It's exhausting to be in a situation where you have to put something forward and you feel like you have to get this man if he's in this position of power or this position of assumed power if he's just jockeying for it to get him to think it's his idea so you can move forward and actually get this thing done.

Women, Gwen notes, are socialized to acknowledge the contributions of others, while men are socialized to take credit away from women and accept it as their own.

In English Studies, we demonstrate, in conference papers, in scholarly articles, in monographs and in textbooks, concern for the sources of ideas. Indeed, there is an entire literature in composition studies dedicated to the study of plagiarism and citation, a literature to which I contributed a substantial amount of work. As I contributed that work, I strove to articulate a disciplinary understanding of plagiarism as the theft not of words but of *credit*. In "Pass It On," I wrote:

> Giving credit to the cited author enacts recognition, a specific form of human wellbeing without which social life would be virtually meaningless. Explaining why theft is wrong and thus why plagiarism is wrong thus requires an examination of precisely what is stolen when someone plagiarizes. The object of the theft, the thing for which the author holds exclusive rights, is not the words or the language or even the ideas, but the *credit*. (419–20)

Though I cannot say with any degree of certainty that this notion of credit as the object of theft ever became commonplace in composition studies, it does indeed stand to reason that what is being stolen is credit. One cannot steal words. When we shift the context from a term paper to a department meeting and we think about what is being stolen when a male colleague hepeats his female colleague's exact words and accepts recognition for those words, it becomes easier to see that what is being stolen is credit. It becomes easier to see that he feels a sense of entitlement to speak and the norms of academic exchange do nothing to preclude that feeling. On the contrary, they encourage it.

Gwen points to a further nuance that often accompanies hepeating. It's not just that a male colleague takes credit for the ideas of a female colleague, but it's also that the audience members seem to see it as a valid concern only once the man articulates it. "The kind of diminishing a person's concern almost like it's because it's their concern. And then having it repeated by a male colleague and having it be a valid concern. Sometimes I'm sitting there and my face must be... what the hell is going on in here?" Another interviewee, Alyssa, also an associate professor at a large public university, points to a similar experience when she tells me that her male colleagues pick up her ideas and present them in ways that she did not, ways that get more traction: "I experience males overly validating you or not validating you at all in meetings. What you say is really important, really good, and then he takes up on that and he expands your ideas and there's mansplaining going on, using fancier words and theoretical embellishments and he presents it in such a good narrative and in such good English, so I think those things are very annoying." One of the effects of this hepeating and this mansplaining is that women like Alyssa end up contributing less to the conversation. As she puts it,

> That's one of the reasons I don't really like talking in department meetings. First, it's very stressful to me—Robert's Rules. I definitely don't like that, but then I've also been in many situations where what I said is exactly what you were saying—either you weren't paying attention to what I was saying or you were really distracted by my accent or the way I was talking—or because I'm female. That really discourages me. I give up. I'm sure someone will say what I'm thinking. It feels really shitty because I want to be a contributing member of the department. I do my work in other areas, but those big meetings are also important—you can make change and also make yourself visible, which is not really my thing anyway, but I know people also use those spaces to make themselves visible in different ways. But it's frustrating. Why do you leave a department meeting feeling like you didn't contribute anything? In your head, you're thinking and doing the work.

Even as Alyssa says she leaves a department meeting feeling like she didn't contribute anything, we can see that she *did* contribute things, but that those things were taken up by men in ways that effaced her contributions.

Erasing Women's Voices in the Graduate Classroom

A second-year doctoral student I'll call Laura tells me that she's angry. "I'm tired of sitting in classes for the past two years and saying something—in most of my classes—and then in twenty minutes I know that a male student will repeat what I said." Male graduate students control the conversation in many graduate classes. Diane, a third-year doctoral student, tells me that because the younger male faculty don't do a very good job controlling "the dominating male voices, other female classmates and I have created a group chat online where we talk and share points and collaborate together during the class and do class work because we can't speak out loud." When female graduate students do speak out loud, they are often dismissed or talked over, as a number of interviewees told me. Caroline, a third-year graduate student, tells me this:

> No matter how much I advocate female scholars or female scholars' theories, it just doesn't really matter if I say it and if there's a man who's accomplished or who proved himself to be very intellectual and advocates one thing about female scholars and it's like, oooh, okay, maybe I should be aware of this women's stuff. Like, I'm sitting right next to you and this white guy just said one thing about the importance of women and you're like, oh, let me be more woke while ignoring what I just said. I don't know what to do with that. Maybe we need that masculine voice to educate other masculine voices, but at the same time it's frustrating.

I tell Caroline about the concept of hepeating. She instantly becomes animated. "Exactly! That happens all the time. How is that not violence? After a while I'm like, whatever I say isn't going to matter, it isn't going to be heard."

Two graduate students told me about male colleagues who refuse to peer review female graduate students' work, and one student I'll call Jeanne told me about a male graduate student who only pays attention when his male colleagues present their work. When his female colleagues present their work, he is on his phone. The graduate students I spoke with understand that their male graduate student colleagues are more heard in classes than they are (Laura: "I think despite the smaller number of men overall, they're much more heard and in terms of opportunities in the department, males get them much more frequently over females"), experience their female friends' ideas being stolen by male graduate student colleagues, and regularly experience being talked over by male colleagues in class.

Beard points in her essay to two exceptions in the classical era to the ban on women speaking: "First, women are allowed to speak out as victims and as martyrs—usually to preface their own death." Manne's work on misogyny calls the legacy of this exception into question, of course, as women who call attention to their experiences with misogyny are, as Manne points out, subject to more misogyny by the lights of patriarchy. The other exception, Beard explains, is that, "occasionally, women could legitimately rise up to speak—to defend their homes, their children, their husbands or the interests of other women." Beard makes clear that we are not "simply the victims or dupes of our classical inheritance, but classical traditions have provided us with a powerful template for thinking about public speech, and for deciding what counts as good oratory or bad, persuasive or not, and whose speech is to be given space to be heard." But female graduate students in doctoral programs in English departments can't even speak about the interests of themselves or other women. A second-year doctoral student I'll call Elizabeth told me two stories about misogyny in graduate classes. The first: "I actually had a male colleague yell at a female colleague to shut up in class one time—having no idea what the intention behind the comment was, but felt that it was his moment to speak, someone else was speaking, this was owed to him." And the second:

> We were having a discussion of whether or not language could be violent. One student was sharing a personal experience—a female student—and a male student responded by completely discounting that experience, basically tromping all over it kind of thing. In another class we were talking about rape culture and a female colleague and myself were discussing our views on the issue and a couple of our male colleagues—again, not in a kind of yes, and sort of way, let me acknowledge your experience and add my experience sort of thing. But just a, "No this is what it is."

Women, in this case, and in many other cases that I heard about, were not allowed to speak publicly in their own interests. And the problem with this statement is that it suggests that rape culture is a women's issue, which it most decidedly is not. But even accepting the commonplace view that it *is* leads us to a place where women are still not allowed a space to speak.

Female graduate students are talked down to (Diane: "I remember the first class I ever took on video games and video game rhetoric. The first question a male peer asked me was where my boyfriend was."), mansplained (Anna: "I had presented different digital humanities projects at different conferences and having someone explain to me what I should be considering when I start a digital humanities project who's never done one and hadn't started working on his yet was really startling") and gaslighted (Amanda: "There's a special kind of gaslighting that's enabled when an academic can claim a scholar-persona that's dedicated to x social justice cause, and that persona is used to invalidate experiential perceptions of that person as a departmental figure/colleague/professor/mentor.") as they work their way through doctoral programs in English. Not only do they not feel heard, but they can see that their male graduate student peers *are* being heard as they are talking over and dismissing female graduate students' contributions to class. And those male graduate students are being heard by faculty who are dealing with and perpetuating the misogyny of silencing in their own lives as faculty in English departments.

Both classroom spaces and faculty meeting rooms are spaces in which knowledge is produced and disseminated; they are, at their best, spaces of collaboration and exchange, and, at their worst, spaces of domination and silencing. What often makes the difference in how such spaces will be experienced by those inhabiting them is their members' conceptualization of epistemic authority: who has the right to claim to know? Manne, in her book *Entitled*, explains that mansplaining "typically stems from an unwarranted sense of entitlement on the part of the mansplainer to occupy the conversational position of the *knower* by default: to be the one who dispenses information, offers corrections, and authoritatively issues explanations" (140). Building on Miranda Fricker's concept of testimonial injustice, wherein a "speaker's word is taken to be less credible than it should be, due to prejudices against members of her social group (for example, as a Black woman) in the relevant domain of knowledge (such as her bodily experiences, pain, illness, and so on)" (140), Manne introduces the concept of epistemic entitlement. "Whereas testimonial injustice involves unfairly dismissing a less privileged speaker—typically, after she has attempted to make a contribution—epistemic entitlement involves peremptorily assuming greater authority to speak, on the part of a more privileged speaker" (141). In the stories we've heard from faculty and graduate students so far, we've witnessed both testimonial injustice and epistemic entitlement; indeed, they seem to happen simultaneously as women are dismissed and as men assume the authority to speak over them, to interrupt them, to correct them, to take credit for their ideas as they hepeat.

In Academic Meetings

I've already shared some women's experiences of having credit for their words and ideas stolen by men who repeat the very things the women have just said, thus engaging in *hepeating*. This is just one of many ways, however, that women faculty in English departments experience their contributions to meetings being erased. So many women spoke to me about being interrupted, talked over, and dismissed in department meetings.

Here's Kelly, a full professor at a regional public four-year university: "In department meetings some of the men who do the smallest amount of interaction and committee work tend to do the most talking and so in many ways they're the most declarative. They are far more likely to diagnose the department without doing anything to try to rectify those situations."

Here's Jill, an associate professor at a Research-1 university: "There are a couple of men in the department, especially older men, some of whom are retired now, who regularly talk over women at department meetings, so it's more behaviors than outright saying incredibly sexist things, as far as my experience of things."

Here's Marie, an instructor at a Research-1 university: "Being interrupted in meetings is the kind of stuff that happens on the daily and most of us don't even pay attention to it anymore. I'm sure it happens daily to me and I probably don't even notice."

And here's Alexandra, an assistant professor at a regional state university: "In a department meeting or any sort of committee meeting, it's dominated by male voices. And I can say they are much more likely to engage in a heated discussion about something and there doesn't seem to be any consequences if they call somebody out on something—it's seen as direct and there's no negativity seen with that."

Men talk in department meetings. Men accept the role of knower, of authority, of epistemic entitlement. Women are there, if they are there for any reason at all, to listen to the men hold forth.

Rebecca, an associate professor at a liberal arts college, spoke for many of the participants in the study when she told me that she felt the pressure to acquiesce to the things men were saying in meetings and that if she couldn't, well, that was her problem: "If you're the person who cannot just nod in a meeting, then that's your problem. It's not the problem of the people that don't want you to talk." And what are women expected to nod along to? For some women I spoke with, it's racist and misogynist content. Here's Susan, an assistant professor at a four-year college that was, until five years ago, a community college, describing department meetings: "There's a lot of sexual content that's really inappropriate. Making comments like, 'Oh, such-and-such student was wearing a really low tank top and that was just'—very much objectifying women and their bodies in a department meeting." Brianna, an assistant professor at a Research-1 university describes meetings at her previous institution, a four-year college:

> [An older male colleague] would make comments about how universities had better students 30 years ago, 40 years ago, and it seemed very obviously racist and sexist. His point of view was that things are going downhill, and he seemed completely unable to recognize that his saying that was saying that he wished he had a bunch of white men to teach.... It was something that the chair wouldn't shut down, so it created this situation where pretty much everyone was stuck listening to him because we didn't know how to shut him down and weren't getting back-up from the chair. We were really frustrated because he kept being given time and space in our meetings to say these things that were clearly racist and sexist.

Lucy, a lecturer at a liberal arts college, tells me what it's like in her department meetings:

> You can tell, like, when one of our new female colleagues contributes in the department meeting that some of our male professors just tune her out. They're just looking at her, waiting for her mouth to stop moving so they can start talking again. That has gotten better over the years, but it still exists. Sometimes it's about—they'll do that to lecturers no matter who it is. Our male lecturers and our female lecturers are on the same level—we used to not be invited to the department meetings and now we are—now we have to go, though we can't really vote on much. When we have something to say, either someone will cut us off and be very assertive to get us to shut up or they'll fold their arms and kind of furrow their brows. After one of the first meetings that we went to, one of my male colleagues came up to me and said, "Now I know what you were talking about. I feel like a woman, too. I didn't say that right." I knew what he meant because we had been talking about misogyny and I was like, you'll never understand because you're not a woman what it's like as a woman and then after the meeting he was trying to tell me, like, I have a little glimpse now, as to what you were talking about. So he didn't say it right, but I knew what he meant. At least he's kind of seeing some things now, too. It's not just me. I can't rage against the machine by myself.

Even as Lucy describes her male colleague getting to the point in a department meeting where he can "see" what some women experience because he, too, as a lecturer, has experienced being silenced, we can see that Lucy is willing to give him the benefit of the doubt as he makes the mistake of saying, "I feel like a woman." "Woman" in his mind is someone who is silenced, dismissed, talked over, undermined. "Woman" is the category into which you place a person whose contributions are not valued. And while, as Lucy put it, he didn't say it right, he's not wrong, at least as far as women faculty's experiences suggest.

It's evident from many of the women that I spoke with that misogyny intersects with rank and that sometimes the reason for the mistreatment is difficult to parse: is it because I'm a woman or because I'm not on the tenure track or both? Moira, an associate professor at a Research-1 university, describes a time during a department meeting when a non-tenure-track faculty member said something important and the tenure-track faculty sat in silence.

> The group of term faculty who are working really hard right now in our department toward more labor equity and the responses to them, it's just uncomfortable silence. People look away, they don't engage, you know, it's this discomfort when they speak up. One of them recently said something that was really important in a meeting, you know, she said the research faculty who have a 2/2 have a 2/2 on their backs. We would not have a 2/2 without their 4/4 and I absolutely agree but she delivered it with such passion and such rage, and I mean they've been fighting for so long and you could just see people sink back, you know, like, withdraw a little bit in their chairs when she said it. I don't know if it would've been different if a man had said it. It's also symptomatic of labor issues, how difficult research faculty find that conversation about labor because we—the latitude of our positions really does rely on the latitude of their positions. But yeah, you could physically see their reactions in the meeting.

The physical reactions of people in meetings to women when they are speaking—as evidenced by Lucy's testimony in which men will fold their arms or furrow their brows waiting for a woman to stop talking, or by Moira's testimony in which tenure-track faculty sink lower in their seats as their female non-tenure-track colleague calls them out on their labor practices—suggest that there is something about women's *voices* themselves that cause people to recoil. Manne points to the debates over Hillary Clinton's voice in March, 2016, and to the fact that people called *her* voice—Kate Manne's—shrill without ever having heard it in order to say that perhaps "we should be suspicious when someone raises this aural specter regarding a woman's voice" (*Down Girl* 285). Perhaps it is, instead, that, as Beard writes, "It doesn't much matter what line you take as a woman, if you venture into traditional male territory, the abuse comes anyway. It's not *what* you say that prompts it, it's the fact that you're saying it."

Silence Creates More Silence

In the epigraph to this chapter, Sady Doyle quotes Adrienne Rich saying that a woman telling the truth creates the possibility for more truth, and Doyle adds to Rich that silence works the same way, that silence works outward in concentric circles. The women who told me stories about being silenced in classrooms and in meetings confirm this; the more they were silenced, the more they self-silenced. The more they were silenced, the less they wanted to speak up in meetings.Recalling Manne's metaphor of misogyny as the shock collar that corrects women who stray from their assigned gender roles, Patricia, an associate professor at an HBCU, tells me, "I feel like I am slowly acquiescing to that shock collar. I no longer want to have ideas at meetings. I sit in meetings and I'm so quiet. I just try to barrel through them."

The women who do speak at meetings do so only after a great deal of careful thought. Moira, who told me about the non-tenure-track faculty in her department speaking up about the tenure-track faculty's 2/2 teaching load, says,

> I think silence and a refusal to engage is typically more the experience I have as a professional if people think I'm speaking out of turn. It's almost a palpable discomfort and so it's hard to say beyond that if you don't receive opportunities because people think what they think—it's hard to know that you haven't received those opportunities. I think the hardest part would be that women who speak their mind are often perceived as angry or brisk and so I'm very careful about when I actually do publicly speak my mind, and when I do, I really feel like it needs to be something worth saying. So for me, I don't know, maybe this is just socialization, I don't speak up a lot in public forums unless I feel very, very strongly about something.

Similarly, Marie tells me, "I think really carefully before I say something. I do have moments where I think about, how is this gonna get perceived, whereas I think there's a real freedom in just saying what you think and not having to think about it."

Pam, a full professor and chair of her department, puts it even more succinctly, "You're shunned for being outspoken." Women know this. They see this all around them. They see their colleagues interrupted, dismissed, subjected to hepeating, and erased altogether. So they remain quiet. And the men speak more. And are heard more. And the norm is reinforced.

Molly left academia not long after I interviewed her for this project in 2019. When I spoke with Molly six weeks after our initial interview, she told me that, though the story I recount in this chapter was a big part of her decision to leave academia, it was not the only reason.

> There were a lot of other factors, too. But, I bet if you traced those factors down to their core, you'd find that, at the root of all of them, is patriarchy. It just got too exhausting for me to continue to do the work I wanted to do within a system that was clearly not designed for my benefit or prosperity. I stayed as long as I could and fought, but I ran out of fight. The main story I told you in my interview was one of the last straws that ground me down so far that it was difficult to care anymore about the work. I decided it was time to find other meaningful work that did not inherently involve my dehumanization and did not constantly require me to be on alert and on the defensive—work that did not require me to constantly defend my own worth and humanity.

Molly did find other, more fulfilling work outside of academia, and she contrasted the culture of her new workplace—a genuinely positive and safe place—with that of her former university. At the start of the 2018–19 school year, the president of her former university "stood in front of our entire faculty and staff and said, 'Take your emotions, bury them, put a smile on your face, and come to work happy no matter what is happening.'"

References

Beard, Mary. "The Public Voice of Women." *London Review of Books* 36.6 (March 2014).
Doyle, Sady. "Nowhere Left to Go." *Believe Me*. Ed. Jessica Valenti and Jaclyn Friedman. New York: Seal Press, 2020. 83–92.
Febos, Melissa. "Thank You for Taking Care of Yourself." *Girlhood*. New York: Bloomsbury, 2021. 193–269.
Manne, Kate. *Down Girl: The Logic of Misogyny*. New York: Oxford UP, 2018.
———. *Entitled: How Male Privilege Hurts Women*. New York: Crown, 2020.
Robillard, Amy E. "Pass It On: Revising the *Plagiarism Is Theft* Metaphor." *JAC* 29.1–2 (2009): 405–435.

2

The Expectation to Serve and Care for Others

> Perhaps the most powerful encouragement for empty consent is that saying no isn't nice.
> —Melissa Febos, "Thank You for Taking Care of Yourself"

> Women are trained to acquiesce to a small request for time, to go to meetings that have no actual agenda, to agree to coffee—to complete the many small labors that we tell ourselves are good for us, will advance our careers, and make us valuable.
> —Carley Moore, "Why I Can't Have Coffee with You"

Jody, a department chair at a community college, tells me a story about a group of men at her school who

> created a faculty group to eat and meet together on Friday afternoons and they didn't realize they only invited men to it and the purpose was to intellectualize the faculty, but they forgot to invite any women. It got kind of shut down pretty quick. Once people higher up started to realize…. They were trying to call it a legitimate campus-wide organization, but they forgot to invite any women to this campus-wide organization, and so when it was reported, and I will say, to the credit of the administration, once it was reported—hey, there's this organization on campus and it's all men with the sole purpose of intellectualizing the faculty and they didn't invite any women—they really shut it down. No, this isn't sanctioned by the college, you haven't gone through any protocols. The administration was like, it is absolutely relevant to have an organization that is dedicated to professional development and larger philosophical questions, but you have to submit by-laws, you have to submit a proposal, you need a budget. Then they invited women to the committee and asked them to do that. Then they wanted to invite women to the committee and they asked them to do that. My colleague was invited. I wasn't invited. I wasn't intellectual enough. My colleague was invited and they asked her and she said no and then the committee, the little group faded away. That was four years ago.

There are a few things that strike me right away about Jody's story, the first among them being that the men in the group invited women only once they were required to. The second, that they invited women to the group and asked them to take care of the administrative duties that they weren't willing to do on their own. And the third, perhaps most striking thing, is that the men were so unwilling to do the administrative work required to keep their group going that it simply faded away.

Jody tells me that she divides the men in her department into two groups—the "men who put out the cookies and the ones who don't." The experience that led to this division, Jody explains, was the time when a male colleague came to her—keep in mind that she is chair of the department—and "asked if I would be willing to partner with him to put on this series of lectures and events" to mark the anniversary of WWII. "I said sure, that would be great, that'd be wonderful."

> So we had a speaker come to campus—typically I've worked with both male and female colleagues, but speaking in terms of misogyny and patriarchy, the job of set-up, break-down, putting out cookies, putting out refreshments, we all work together, we all break it all down, and then you go out and eat with the speaker. When I said, hey, can you put out the cookies, he said, I don't know how to do that. That's why it's our joke now at work—I like this person because he'll put out the cookies. He came in, engaged with the speaker, and then when it was over, left with the speaker to go to dinner and didn't invite anybody to join him and left us standing there to break it all down. By then it was too late. I was in February of this year-long project, and I'm like, we're gonna finish it because my name's attached to it now and I want it to look good, but I've never worked with that faculty member again. And that's how we got the phrase—when he told me he didn't know how to put out the cookies, I was like, oh my gosh. If I don't know how to do it, you won't make me do it.

Service in the academy has not always been linked with administrative or what Jody calls "housekeeping" work; as Leonard Cassuto explains, university service first emerged as a concept opposed to research at the turn of the twentieth century, though it was a service focused primarily on the public rather than on the university itself. The principal question was "what role the university ought to play in society at large." It wasn't until the 1920s that the familiar teaching-research-service triad first appeared, Cassuto explains, and this was largely a result of the concept of the credit hour bureaucratizing higher education and "dividing professors' work into categories." Further, the rise of the department created a need for the kind of service we understand today as university service "because service was needed by department heads to make departments run." With the Cold War and the increasing need to publish more, faculty were encouraged to focus more and more on their disciplinary careers—the work we do as members of our academic disciplines—and less on their institutional careers—the work we do to maintain our institutions—with university service falling into the most devalued of the familiar triad. Despite any number of arguments for the intellectual value of service, we are left with this devaluing today, as Cassuto puts it, "until a seismic higher educational event occurs."

I need not do a review of the literature to persuade you that work that is devalued in any sector becomes, de facto, women's work. Indeed, there have been any number of studies of the gendered distribution of labor with respect to academic service (e.g., O'Meara; Park; Masse and Hogan). Manne reminds us that in a patriarchy, it is a woman's job to *give*, and one of the things she is expected to give is *care* for others; she is expected to tend to all things, living and non, to maintain homeostasis in systems, and to do so with nobody noticing. Perhaps what is most notable about the way women are expected to give in the realm of academic service is that it simply *expected* that they will do it and they will do it well; at the same time, it is simply *expected* that men will not do it and that when they do it, they will do it poorly.

In this chapter, I share women's stories about service expectations for men and women in their English departments. It is important to note that I did not ask a specific question about university service in the course of my interviews, but the subject came up so many times that I could not help but devote space and time to it in this work. The women I spoke with felt pressure to take on more service than they could do at the same time that they saw the men around them getting out of service commitments or doing it so poorly that nobody wanted them to do it for fear they would just create more problems. Men seemed to experience a sense of entitlement to exemption from service work while women felt an inability to say no even when asked to do an inequitable amount of labor. In the words of Miranda, a full professor at a small liberal arts college, "Women are supposed to be responsible and men are allowed to behave with learned helplessness."

Men's Entitlement to Exemption from Service

To *get away with* something is to escape consequence, to avoid punishment for having done something wrong. When women spoke with me about men not doing service, a few of them used the language of men *getting away with* not doing service, and, in the framework of misogyny that I'm using here—give and take, reward and punishment—it is instructive to contrast the idea of men getting away with not doing service with the case of a woman not doing her share of service in a department. How would she be treated? In what ways would she be punished? One way we know she will be treated is that she will have male colleagues disparaging her in meetings. Gwen tells me about a colleague who was "going around talking to other colleagues about me and my salary and how he feels like I shouldn't be getting paid more than he does. That actually being said in a meeting—there were certain comments that were said directly about me and the ways in which I've been engaging or not able to this last year—these last couple years have been very difficult for me." When her colleague believed she wasn't pulling her weight, so to speak, her salary was called into question and she was disparaged by name in meetings. What happens to men who don't seem to be pulling their weight?

"The way we deal with it in our department," says Moira, "is that we occasionally—only occasionally—talk about experiences with a couple key players who, for whatever reason, just seem to get away with murder. I won't say murder. They get away with the absolute bare minimum. I want that life."

Moira continues,

> My experience is that the men just don't show up. When they work, they don't work as hard. They compartmentalize an awful lot of things and tend to overlook. The other thing is I think some of them would be shocked if I were to say something to them about that, right? "You strike me as somebody who's not really present." "Well, what do you mean by that? I'm here all the time. I've published five so-and-sos." Well, yeah, but somebody else did all the shit work.

Again and again, women told me about the men in their departments just not doing the service work, finding ways to get out of it, feigning helplessness.

Here's Jody again, using her cookies phrasing: "The women tend to put out the cookies, doing the heavy lifting, doing the emotional labor, you know, the kind of day-to-day housekeeping tasks that keep a department running and, historically, some of the men in the department have been able to get by without doing that."

Here's Rebecca, an associate professor at a liberal arts college: "Men don't volunteer. For example, we have to do program review, and out of my five colleagues, the men were just like, 'Nah, we don't have time, we're already planned out for the next ten years.' That's a typical thing that happens all the time. They're finishing a book or they have grandchildren or whatever, but it always goes around like this. 'We don't have to do this because you guys will pick up the slack.'"

Here's Elizabeth, a non-tenure-track instructor at a mid-sized public university: "On the committees that I've served on, the immediate response to leadership has been men stepping up to take care of those leadership roles and looking to women on the committees to serve as secretaries."

Here's Kelly, a full professor at a regional four-year university: "I would say [gender roles] are fairly traditional in that in committee work women do most of the actual grunt work. They are more inclined to be the people in charge of putting together documents, even though they may be the idea people. The men tend to think of themselves as the idea people and don't do the writing that goes along with that or the organization that goes along with that. I don't believe there's an equal bar for men and women as far as service is concerned."

Here's Alexandra, an assistant professor at a regional state university: referring to an overextended female colleague, "I can't think of a single man in our department who's overextended in the same way. Because they're like, oh, I only have to do this many committees to be good for tenure? Then that's what I'm doing. They don't feel compelled to do more."

Here's Sara, a senior lecturer at a private Research-1 university: "There is a general sense among the female faculty in this department that they are often called to do service that men are not called upon to do. When somebody in the department needs help, it's always the women who provide rides or bring meals or all of that stuff. I think there's also a sense that women frequently get stuck at the associate professor level because they do so much service."

Graduate students, too, notice the disparities between the amount of service men and women do. Here's Eva, a first-year doctoral student in creative writing at a public Research-2 university: "Women have the public face positions of power, but behind the scenes it's men running everything and men getting away with being mediocre."

Here's Beth, a third-year doctoral student at a public university: "Male graduate students are less likely to volunteer or take on assistantships that require administrative duties. When they do volunteer for service roles, their performance in those roles is negligent. Female or women-identifying faculty take on more service roles in the department, chairing committees and starting up new initiatives, especially assistant or associate professors. Female graduate students are also more likely to volunteer and take on assistantships that require administrative duties."

And here's Anna, a doctoral student who is ABD in creative writing at a state university: "I have noticed in some of my friends' experiences when they're on committees with men and women where the man who's on the committee has received emails from the professors thanking him for all his hard work when he doesn't have a leadership role and ccing the two other women on the committee, but not mentioning them, whereas I lived with one of the women, so I know how much work she did and she worked really hard. Seeing things like this happen is pretty disheartening and makes it clear that there are certain things like authority or leadership that are coded as being masculine, so when there's a mixed group of individuals, it's the man who's in charge without working harder, necessarily."

Patricia, an associate professor at an HBCU, tells me a story about being placed on the curriculum committee her first year and then, after telling her chair that she was pregnant, being removed from the curriculum committee and placed on the hospitality committee, which "is birthdays and cupcakes and was made up of two pregnant women and a woman who was having a disability issue." In the four years Patricia has been at her institution, she tells me,

> I have not been able to shake that committee. Any time a man is nominated for that committee, he is off it within hours. And when I started getting recognition for doing a good job on that committee, they cut my budget entirely. There is no more budget for it, but I'm still expected to do duties for it. I'm not allowed to bring food in from home, but I'm supposed to have snacks and things like that. It is just this catch-22. My chairperson did call me in and yell at me because I wasn't doing enough for that committee. This is while I'm seven months pregnant and the other faculty member was eight or nine months pregnant and the other faculty member was going blind. I have suggested revamping it as a social media committee, a branding committee, anything other than June Cleaver cupcakes and pearls and I have gotten absolutely no traction through two chairpeople.

Though it is, of course, worth noting that there is no inherent connection between pregnancy and hospitality, I also want to point out that Patricia makes clear in her story that men do not serve on the hospitality committee. When they are appointed to it, they are "off it within hours."

Men feign helplessness, point to their scholarship, do the bare minimum, expect women to take up the slack, and, in some cases, refuse to do service altogether, blaming women for being too emotional. Theresa tells me a story of something that happened on her writing committee when a junior male colleague "decided, as one person put it, he would just throw a bomb in the middle of our committee." Theresa continues:

> He accused three of us—the three senior women faculty—of deliberately trying to be inefficient in meetings and not make decisions. It was just ridiculous. He took emails out of context—emails we had all received—and pieced them together so they said different things and accused of us being emotional, dismissing emotional labor within meetings. So, for example, if our composition director came in and there was something that had happened and she needed to talk about it with us, that was inappropriate. We should be using Robert's Rules of Order to function. We've never, ever functioned that way.... We had to go through this stupid mediation that didn't work. He did it in early February and all meetings were halted. He refused to come to meetings. We didn't meet. He had this ridiculous list of rules he wanted us to abide by. He even accused us of making faces at him. It was ridiculous. He wanted to not have to come, to not be included on any group email, not come to any meetings, and if we needed anything, he'd be happy to participate, but we had to come to him individually. And all of us are like, there's no fucking way we're gonna come individually. So we're gonna have our meeting and then summarize it for him? It still makes me sick.

In Theresa's story we see a startlingly egregious case of a man expressing his sense of entitlement to remain exempt from department service, his entitlement being grounded in his claim that the women on the committee were being too emotional. While Manne points to patriarchy's requirement that women provide care and nurturing to others and expect no care and nurturing in return, patriarchy also punishes women who demonstrate too much care. When a woman gives *too much care* and the man in question is not on the receiving end of that care, that woman is understood to be weak and *emotional*. About her male colleague, Theresa says, "There's not going to be an easy solution to everything that you can just vote on. You have to get in that mess sometimes. I think he just wants to vote on everything and check it off a list."

Brianna, an assistant professor and Writing Program Administrator (WPA) at a Research-1 university, describes the differences between her experience as WPA and what she sees male WPAs doing.

> At my previous institution I was the WPA, and I'm the WPA here too, but at my previous institution, I had no hiring or firing abilities and my chair, who was a man, was very clear that I wasn't the one in charge of those decisions, so it was very clear to me that I could and was expected to take on a lot of the caring, mentoring, sheltering of the TAs during their program. One of the creative writers, she had a really similar role, she was an associate professor, and she and I both worked really closely with a lot of the graduate students—it was really frustrating because it felt like we were constantly doing the caring, constantly doing all kinds

of emotional labor that other people in the department weren't expected to do, and I think the frustration there was also sort of being expected to do this emotional labor without being given the authority to actually intervene if there was a legitimate problem. That was honestly one of the reasons I left. I think it's been interesting in the WPA position at my current institution—I still think a WPA, especially a woman WPA ends up doing a lot of that care work in ways that even my male friends who are WPAs just don't—aren't expected to do. I think in my department there are men who take on some of that work, but they get away with not being as involved with students and other faculty members.

There's that language again: men *get away with* not doing as much service, with not being as involved with others. Brianna continues:

I think the men are able to get away with things but I don't know that they think about it very often, but I don't know how to explain that further. Maybe at the assistant professor level, what seems to happen, the women, as we know is typical, tend to take on more service duties or just be more involved with students, where I feel like the assistant professors who are men have a much easier time saying, "I'm just gonna go do my research and teach my classes." Some of the women may want to take on that work, but the men are just, "I'm gonna go write my book that I need."

Another way to think about what men are getting away with when they don't do the requisite amount of service work in their departments is *saying no*. They have, as we have seen here, many ways of saying no to service: they point, most often, to their research. Or they take note of the minimum number of committees they need to serve on and they do that. Or they even point to family commitments, as Rebecca noted. What they don't do, it seems, is second-guess their ability to say no because they understand that women will overextend themselves, that women will take up the slack. As Lisa, an assistant professor on a STEM-focused campus, tells me about a particular woman on her campus whom I'll call Janet:

Janet is viewed positively by most of the women in the department and is often—she's very much not valued by males in the department. Coming back to that service issue—if something needs to be done, "Oh, well, Janet can just do it." It's this idea that, especially this particular woman who's unmarried and older and doesn't have children, that it's just assumed that she can be the one to take care of things, especially if it's a job that's not highly valued in some way. "That's okay, they'll do it. They'll take care of it." I think that's true, too, of other women in the department, particularly those of us who—and this is kind of on the other end of the spectrum, but who are young and new and building our careers and are also local—we're the ones who end up doing all of the things that need to be done and all of the undesirable tasks, whereas many of the men in particular are the ones the work doesn't end up falling on.

Why do men believe that women will take care of it? Because men know that women have been socialized to not say no. Men know that women have been socialized to be nice, to take into account other people's feelings, and that, as Melissa Febos writes in the context of sexual consent, "perhaps the most powerful encouragement for empty consent is that saying no isn't nice" (234).

On Feeling Unable to Say No

Who in a department is allowed to say no without consequence? Who is allowed to get away with saying no? Saying no indicates agency, empowerment, control over one's time and energy. Saying no goes against everything women have been socialized to believe about themselves in a patriarchy: we are here to serve others, to please others, to make others' lives easier. When someone asks us to do something, we should do it and if we cannot do it, we should apologize profusely. Even if—especially if?—we are not required to do that work. Does it matter what she says no to?

> What about the times when she fails to provide feminine-coded goods and services, in the right way, at the right time? Withholding sympathy makes her a bitch; looking inward makes her cold or selfish; being ambitious makes her hostile and anti-social, as well as untrustworthy (Hellman et al. 2004); giving sexual attention to the wrong person makes her a slut—or a dyke, an unsexy lesbian; if she was wearing the wrong thing, or drunk, she was asking for it. Or, she led him on. She prevailed on him to take what was promised to him, sexually: what he had coming. (Manne *Down Girl* 296).

As any search for "women saying no," as well as Manne's work here, indicates, the realm in which women are most unable to say no is sexual; women are expected to give of their bodies first and foremost (more on this in Chapter 4). But that expectation that women don't say no extends into the workplace, especially one in which the work women do is by its very nature *giving*. Advice columns and memes help academics learn how to say no, even if our mentors do not. They suggest weighing the pros and cons of an opportunity, practicing with friends the hard no and the maybe, and suggesting to the asker a more qualified colleague for the task. They provide templates for saying no, asking you to fill in the blanks by saying, "Right now I'm busy with _____ and _____, and am unable to take on additional service." What the advice columnists and memes do not consider, as far as I can tell, is gender and guilt.

Marie, a non-tenure-track instructor at a public Research-1 university, described the problem with saying no to service this way:

> In the department, I see most of the labor in terms of service that goes beyond required committees being relegated to women or not even relegated—women are the first people asked to do it and men seem to be farther down the list. Also, in just talking to people, I see women having a harder time saying no when asked to do some of those things. There seems to be—entitlement seems to be the right word—there seems to be an acceptance of my male colleagues saying no and being okay with saying no and not feeling a sense of guilt surrounding that. For example, I know that if there's ever something extra that needs to be done on a committee that I'm on, nine times out of ten, there's this awkward silence and then it's a woman who steps up and says, "Okay, I'll do it," and the men on the committee just sort of sit there.

Theresa tells me that she recognized the problem with her inability to say no and did something about it:

> I was told I have to sit on this committee because there's no one else, and I just wonder how far down the list my chair went before she came to me and said that and how likely I am to say no compared to someone else. I think that is really common, to the point where I had a "no" buddy last year and we would try to support each other in saying no so that we wouldn't always get pulled into those kinds of service expectations. Or taking on work that someone else could easily take on.

Marie says, "Just being able to say no is a huge thing," and Brianna demonstrates that sometimes the only way a woman can say no is when she is so overloaded with other work that it is physically impossible to do more:

> I will say I do have an older male faculty member and he's not overly misogynistic but we did have a meeting and we have a program and it's kind of neglected at this point and so there's three women in my department—none of us have tenure yet and we all have pretty heavy administrative roles. So we were talking about this program and he said something like, "Somebody just needs to get passionate

about it, blah blah blah, somebody just needs to take on this work," and we were like, "We can't. We just don't have time." He could, but he won't volunteer to and so to me it just seems like a typical example of him wanting us to volunteer to take on this work when he clearly would be one of the people who should take on the work because he doesn't already have all the service work.

But as I intimated above when I suggested that we work in a caring profession, saying no is not just a problem with service. Saying no is also difficult when we have internalized the expectation that we will play the nurturing role as teachers and givers.

The word "mother" came up a few times in my interviews, as I talked with women about their understandings of others' expectations of them. Gwen puts it this way:

> It's like, in each area, how you do your service, how you teach, how you do your scholarship, it's like you're supposed to be mothering, and what if you don't feel like doing that? What if this is not a good time, you don't have the bandwidth to do it? It's like, there's the shock collar that's like, well, no, the way you're supposed to do it is supposed to look like this and you're supposed to have never-ending patience and compassion no matter how much of an ass this person might act—this student might act, this colleague might act, this supervisor might act—you're supposed to have never-ending patience. There should never be a time when you actually raise your voice. And if you're going to be upset, you should cry.

Dorothy, a professor emerita at a Research-2 university, tells me, "I've always had this tension between knowing where the power lies and being able to use it and exercise it but feeling that I ought to be playing that nurturing role. I've always felt like I should, but even as a mother I'm not very good at it. I'm just not made for that role. I've often felt guilty. It's one of the reasons I wanted to talk about this. I'm just not the mommy type."

Elizabeth, an instructor at a public university, explains that she feels pressure to mother her students: "Very frequently you hear a lot of, particularly in that kind of care and mothering description of, what are you doing to take care of your students, that you tend not to hear with male colleagues quite so much. So we're the ones that are frequently asked to be a part of welcoming groups and how do we make students feel like they are a part of this family—and you'll hear that language a lot within the department itself—we are this family." And it's not just undergraduate students who seem to expect this type of mothering. As Moira explains, "I would say that the dynamic of that sort of gendered structure where we are required as women to be emotionally supportive, mothering, is an omnipresent experience in our work. It's not just with graduate students. I sort of expect it with undergrads, but with my graduate students, I'm thinking, well, you know you signed up to build a career as a professional, so there's gonna be some challenge here, right?"

It's not just colleagues who expect women to live up to the nurturing stereotype; the women I spoke with told me that it's the expectations coming from students that put a lot of pressure on them to play the role of nurturer. As Bonnie, a full professor at a public Research-2 university, puts it, "If a female professor doesn't do these things, give lots of chances, isn't warm and forgiving and nurturing and all that—students complain when the male professors aren't like that, too, but it seems to happen more with women, especially women of color." Similarly, Rebecca says, "The students are all sitting in classes and they're expecting women to act like male professors and mothers at the same time, ideally. It becomes like this—you're not just the caregiver of the department, you're the caregiver of the one hundred and something students you're teaching each semester, and those are the students who are coming to *you* when there's a problem and not their male professor, and so there's a lot of emotional labor." And Marie tells me this story:

> I had one student who said—this just happened in the spring—he said he thought it was really unacceptable that I didn't reach out to him when he had a failing grade on a midterm essay and that he thought that fell so far outside of the realm of the work that he had been doing for the course and why wouldn't I reach out to him and ask him what was wrong?... He felt very entitled to tell me that I should have reached out to him and that he used to coach a sports team and that that was a sign of a good coach and that I should care more. I should care more, that was one of the things he said. I should care more about my students. So that felt really patronizing.

Women are not students' mothers, and we are not students' therapists, as Alyssa points out with her efforts to say no to students: "I've been trying to—I've been better at saying, no, this isn't my place, or, no, I don't want to work with you, I'm not your therapist. But when that happens with colleagues, I can't always do the same thing." It may be a bit easier to say no to students, as Alyssa points out, but colleagues and supervisors still expect women to go above and beyond when it comes to teaching. Michelle, a professor and chair of her department at a community college, tells me about the requirements to care outside of teaching hours:

It's become an unofficial requirement not only to teach but also to be the therapist and also, if someone's having trouble finding a solution to their problems, be that sympathetic ear. I've actually stayed until 11 or 12 at night trying to help a student even though my class ended at 9 because you're supposed to go above and beyond and spend that extra time. While specific things aren't encouraged, it is encouraged that you spend a little more one-on-one time, be a little more—I want to say compassionate, but it's not really compassionate because it's going beyond the basics of compassion. It feels a little awkward if you don't want to do it or if other people are doing it and you're not, there's that undertone of, well, you should be because you care.

If you care, you won't say no. This is what so many women in academia are made to believe. This is what so many women in *so many aspects of life* are made to believe, but it is particularly pernicious in academia, where we come to the work in the first place because we care about it, because we want to make a difference in our fields and in the lives of our students. And while it may seem easy enough to tell others to just say no to the additional requests, to provide formulas and tips for *how* to say no and *when* to say no, it's not quite so easy to undo years and years of socialization that tells us that saying no isn't nice. And we have to be nice or others won't like us.

At least a few of the women I spoke with have begun learning how to say no. Rebecca tells me,

> Another woman in my department is currently taking up all sorts of service work on the side because men are not picking it up, which is a situation where she's already running a grant and some other stuff, but of course she volunteers for the large summer project because nobody else does it. I have to say, I used to do that, too, until I realized that I was the only person actually working on this all summer long without any recognition for that.

Kelly, a full professor at a regional university, tells me that, though she considers herself very involved in her department, "I do find myself asking, 'Wait, am I going above and beyond in a way that I am really *choosing* to go above and beyond—as opposed to doing so reflexively?' That is a thing that was not in my brain five years ago, but it is now." And Alexandra tells me that, having moved across the country following a terrible work experience,

> I'm at a place where if somebody asks me to do something, my immediate response—I don't say this out loud, necessarily, but my immediate response is, what do I get for it? It killed my generosity of spirit in a good way and in a bad

way. There's a part of me that's like, I am a nurturing, giving person and I like to help people out, but in a good way now, I'm much more selective in how I do that work. I think it necessarily has to be that way, so I'm—even this grant work I'm doing next fall—they're offering me money to do it. It's not a ton of money, but it does add up. That's my new approach to things—unless I'm getting something for this, I'm not doing this out of the kindness of my heart anymore.

English departments are microcosms of patriarchal society; no matter how much discourse we churn out declaring our allegiance to diversity, equity, and inclusion, departments are still made up of people who have internalized beliefs about who should do what kinds of work, who should serve whom, and who should care for the most fragile among us. Dislodging beliefs about who is allowed to say no with what consequences will take more than storytelling, but storytelling is where we must begin. We must first be willing to see and hear the truth about who is doing what work to keep departments running and to keep students on track, and we must be willing to question why so many women are overextended. We must be willing to listen to them when they say no.

References

Cassuto, Leonard. "University Service: The History of an Idea." *Profession*, Nov. 2016.
Febos, Melissa. "Thank You for Taking Care of Yourself." *Girlhood*. New York: Bloomsbury, 2021. 193–269.
Manne, Kate. *Down Girl: The Logic of Misogyny*. New York: Oxford UP, 2018.
Masse, Michelle A., and Katie J. Hogan, Eds. *Over Ten Million Served: Gendered Service in Language and Literature Workplaces*. Albany: SUNY Press, 2010.
O'Meara, Kerryann. "Whose Problem Is It? Gender Differences in Faculty Thinking About Campus Service." *Teachers College Record* 118 (2016): 1–38.
Park, Shelley M. "Research, Teaching, and Service: Why Shouldn't Women's Work Count?" *Journal of Higher Education* 67.1 (1996): 46–84.

3

Masculine-Coded Goods in English Departments: Respect, Authority, Leadership

Girls grow up in a world hostile to female intelligence, but the academy is supposed to be a bastion against anti-intellectualism. It isn't. In academia as outside it, female students tend not to receive their fair share of encouragement, and often they are confronted with outright skepticism about their abilities.

—Troy Vettese, "Sexism in the Academy"

If you are a male and you know how to use words in such a way to assert authority and power, that gives you an edge up on a woman whose way to assert authority is by kindness and gentleness.

—Sara, Senior Lecturer

Jill, an associate professor at an R-1 university, tells me a story about being hired by her institution to run the writing program only to learn, once she got there, that the offer had changed and she was now being offered the position of associate director,

> with my role being a course coordinator, which is a job that had typically been assigned to graduate students. My response was, "I've been an associate director of an Ivy League writing program; that's insulting." So I was pretty firm. Two weeks later the offer was repeated to me as if it had not been made before, but it's also created a rift between me and the director. The chair took the director's side of it. I was actually told I should go in and visit Bob [the writing director] in his office just to talk. Just in general, I should be nicer to him. I said, "He is free to come to my office any time." That never happened. And I was essentially told that I was being offered the job of associate director and that was my role and I should take it and I refused. That has definitely created a rift with me and the former chair and her allies. But I just wouldn't do that. I wouldn't work under Bob. I would have been happy to work with him, but that wasn't the offer.

When faced with a bait-and-switch, Jill doesn't back down but instead refuses to be associated with the writing program at all, despite being told by her chair that she should "be nicer" to the writing program director. Her role, she is told, is to work under the director, not *as* the director despite having been hired to be the director. When she asks for the masculine-coded goods to which she is entitled by virtue of her years of experience and her contract, she is told to be nice. When she invites Bob to come talk to her, nothing happens. As a result, Jill tells me, "I redirected my career towards medical humanities—still with an interest in writing, work in writing, but focused toward the medical humanities so I could have a career."

In this chapter, I share stories women told me about asking for and being refused masculine-coded goods such as respect, authority, and salary, and I identify the punishments they endured for having asked for such goods. In these stories, we see women asking for goods that are, in a patriarchy, understood to be his alone for the taking: "leadership, authority, influence, money, and other forms of power, as well as social status, prestige, rank, and the markers thereof" (Manne, *Down Girl* 113). Sometimes women just take them, rather than asking for them, and often, women are punished by being shocked back into place: being given more work to do, not getting the promotion, being questioned about their capabilities, being characterized as aggressive or too assertive. And women know these things; they know how the stories go when a woman asks for something she is not entitled to. The story will end with punishment. This becomes most clear when Elizabeth, a non-tenure-track lecturer working toward her Ph.D., tells me that she hadn't experienced much misogyny personally

> because I haven't attempted to step into any leadership roles because I'm an adjunct and because, a couple years ago when I decided to start working on this Ph.D., I stepped out of any extra things that I was doing at work because there's only so much time in the day.... Because I haven't stepped into those leadership positions, I haven't put myself in a position to receive that direct attack.

By *not* asking for an obviously masculine-coded good like leadership, Elizabeth believes she has saved herself from direct misogynistic attacks. The rules of the patriarchy are understood by all: do not ask for that which you are not entitled to. Continue to give what you are obligated to give. When you break these rules, expect to be punished.

Respect, Authority, and Leadership Are Masculine-Coded Goods

Several women I spoke with shared with me their understanding that respect, authority, and leadership are goods that men are automatically assumed to possess and, if they do not possess them, most people in the department believe that they *should*. Manne characterizes respect, authority, and leadership as masculine-coded goods to which men are entitled in a patriarchy and which women should not request as long as men see them as valuable (*Down Girl* 113). Lisa, an assistant professor at a STEM-focused campus, tells me about a meeting with a bunch of male professors.

> There was a person from educational technology running the meeting. And whenever that person would refer to one of the men in the room, they would say, Dr. So-and-so, Dr. So-and-so, and then when it came to referring to me, I was just Lisa, which I found to be—I mean, it's a microaggression, and I don't think this person has anything against me, he probably didn't even realize he was doing it, but at the same time, it's this environment where the respect and the authority automatically goes to men.

The assumption in the room is that the men deserve titles and the woman should be referred to by her first name, the familiar address.

Gwen observes the way, in her department, men's and women's scholarship is treated differently:

> There's a kind of coded way of talking about the work that people do that will aggrandize the work that the man is doing and diminish the work that a female colleague is doing. And sometimes that happens in subdisciplinary ways. It'll usually be like, my work in this area or the work of these male colleagues in this area is more important than this other area because our work is reasonable, rational, coded in these very Enlightenment, masculine ways. And feminizing and diminishing another subdiscipline or the work that people are doing in that subdiscipline or concerns, for example, about ideology and methodology and some of the things we're teaching about, and some of the concerns we might want students to have about, say, identity and markers of identity and saying that those things aren't important because white men aren't talking about them. So they're multiply coded. It's not just gender. It's also race, and sexuality, and class.

Men's scholarship is what matters, and men's scholarship is what deserves the attention and respect of the department. Sara, a senior lecturer at a Research-1 private university, echoes Gwen's sentiment when she tells me that her chair,

> who actually makes an effort to be compassionate and try to be aware of what's going on, constantly overlooks female faculty accomplishments. Now, when it's pointed out to him, he tries to make up for that, but he will in my conversations with him say things like, "Well, you know, I won a Guggenheim." And it's like, I never hear the female faculty talking about themselves in those terms. And he is not alone among the male faculty here who talk like this marker is something that identifies me. We need to put a medal around your neck. Hard not to laugh, but he's very serious. It gives him insight into the world that others don't have.

I couldn't help but laugh when Sara told me this, of course, but it is also important to point out that it doesn't occur to her chair to acknowledge female faculty members' accomplishments—it must be pointed out to him that he has overlooked them. Only then will this otherwise "compassionate" chair recognize the work of women. He needs no such prodding to recognize the work of the men in his department.

Two women told me about men in their departments who believe they should be in leadership positions instead of the women who actually were in those positions. Elizabeth works with a man

> who believes that he should have a particular leadership role, that he's the only person who should have this role and he literally explicitly stated it in those exact terms and right now there is a woman in that role and his reaction has been really kind of outrageous in terms of, "She's not qualified. I am qualified. I have these things. I deserve this respect and leadership and so forth." He has very clearly expressed how he feels that this is his and it should be his and he is owed it, which is really bizarre. You see a fair amount of that in terms of, my way of doing things is right. I deserve this respect and deferential treatment, almost.

And Miranda, who is professor and department chair at a small liberal arts college, tells me that she has a colleague who believes *he* should be department chair.

> He's an irascible somebody, to put it politely, and lurks up in the third floor and doesn't come to department meetings—he hasn't been to a department meeting in three years, since I came here—and I'm meeting with every member of the faculty and I'm asking them about leadership of the department and I'm asking

everybody the same questions and he says he'd be happy to be chair. And I'm thinking, excuse me. Just please excuse me.

The men in these two instances have no compunction about expressing their entitlement to leadership positions because they understand that leadership is coded male. If women had done something similar in either case, they likely would have been promptly punished with any number of down-girl moves.

Graduate students, too, notice the ways men are presumed to be the bearers of authority and leadership. Laura, a third-year doctoral student at a Research-2 university, tells me about a time when a male graduate student received intellectual credit for work he had not done:

> I'm thinking specifically of my year on the writing program team. It was all females and one male. I was able to see in the orientation process the females were all paired up with individuals to go over course plans. We would mentor them, and it was a lot of emotional labor because not only were we going through the peculiar aspects of each course plan, but we were also talking about the curriculum, how they saw themselves as teachers, and in that entire process, I can't think of one instance that the male student was actually doing that work. But I do recall that, despite that—and this was one of the most emotionally taxing things I've ever done—one of the students was like, that male student was really my mentor during that process, even though I know that he was not in the room when we were doing that.

Anna, a doctoral candidate at a Research-2 university, tells me a story about a male graduate student colleague quit the literary magazine over a request she made.

> I was co-editor-in-chief for a couple years with someone—he's really great—but I noticed that people were way less inclined to do things when I asked them to do it and we even had one person quit being on the literary magazine because we've had something in place that predated us where everyone who was an editor or assistant editor needed to write one blog post for the magazine website per year. So it's like five hundred words, really not an extensive project, and it was in place before we took over, and we started just kind of making it more formal, where there's a schedule…and this one person hadn't signed up or done anything and I sent them a reminder email. "Hey, can you sign up, there's still some slots available and I noticed your name wasn't on the list." And they ended up getting really upset saying that we shouldn't have anything mandatory and he quit. And then he called my co-editor-in-chief later that day to say, "Hey, I'm really sorry,

I didn't mean to be harsh. I'm just under a lot of stress," and I was like, oh god. Why are you apologizing to *him*?

In Anna's story, we see that her male graduate student colleague understood apologies to be something his male colleague deserved, but not his female colleague, the person who he actually insulted with his rushed exit from the magazine. Who deserves the respect of a reconsideration? "It really felt like there was this one-sided ray of anger coming at me and I couldn't really tell why," Anna tells me.

Caroline, a third-year doctoral student at a Research-2 university, tells me that she hears new graduate students complaining about the women in leadership positions in her department. "I hear stories that people, new students, are complaining, this is such a female-oriented department, women obviously feel like they get to run this department, so probably what they think is that these masculine goods like authority and leadership are supposed to be male. Women are doing this, so that's bad, and it should be considered wrong."

Finally, women noticed the different expectations colleagues and students have for their own and their male colleagues' *dress*. If women have to pay attention to their clothing in order to encourage respect, but men do not, it stands to reason that men are presumed to earn respect by virtue of being men.

Here's Marie, a non-tenure-track instructor at a public Research-1 university:

> What jumps out at me is the way that my male colleagues dress vs. the way my female colleagues dress. The men are, by and large, more casual, wearing stuff that I don't even think would fall under casual Friday—more like bumming around your house on the weekend. That jumps out at me because I think to myself, wow, it must be really great to be able to stand in front of the class and not be judged because you're wearing crappy jeans and a t-shirt that looks like you just pulled out of a pile. If I did that, I think I would be judged very differently.

Here's Jackie, a doctoral candidate at a public Research-2 university:

> The emphasis on femme, feminine dress and the fact that I will wear ties and button-downs, it's not, it shouldn't be a big deal, but there are faculty that will outright stare at me. I feel like I'm in a zoo.
>
> I get comments from female faculty like, "Why did you cut off all your hair? You looked so pretty." It was super weird. I'm like, I really like my hair the way it is now. You don't have to say anything.... I have seen male graduate students teach in gym shorts. I'm like, really, you have something to say to me about this, about the fact that I'm wearing a bow tie, are you kidding me? I do feel like I've stepped back in time a little bit.

And here's Laura, a third-year doctoral student at a Research-2 university:

> When I first got here I remember I was at a bar with some older students who'd been in the program longer and one of them was like, "I want you to know"—it was a male student—"I want you to know that the only way your students are going to respect you is if you wear a collar." After that, he said he was joking and I was like, "Excuse me?" But I think I still internalized that because I dress up a lot to teach and that's a thing I think I do for me because I care about clothes and I care about how I present myself but also sometimes I wish that I didn't have to. I see that my male peers do not and many other female peers don't either. I think my level of formality is a way that I build distance.

Men *look* the part simply by presenting as male, and women have to pay special attention to their clothing—wearing collars, perhaps—to garner some of the respect men seem to know they don't have to work for.

When Women Want Intellectual Authority, Salary, Promotions

Lisa tells me a story about a research project she launched on campus to students, faculty, and staff about language attitudes.

> I asked them to listen to some audio clips of some people speaking and to respond to some questions about these people like, how friendly do you think they are and how intelligent do you think they are, those kinds of things.... There were also a number of very specific demographic questions asking things like, what is your native language and are you from the U.S. or not and where are you from and what's your age, those kinds of things, because I'm looking for potential correlations to language attitudes.

Lisa explains to me that she and her two colleagues—one, a professor in the psychology department, and one an undergraduate researcher—took a long time putting the survey together and were very careful with its design. On the day after the survey went out to faculty,

> I got two different messages from two different male professors, both of them in the engineering school, very pointed emails suggesting that my survey was not as anonymous as I had suggested that it was because the demographic questions were too specific. Essentially saying that if I wanted to, I could put all the pieces

> together of somebody's responses and figure out who they were. The way these emails were worded, though, were very, very pointed and very much not what you would expect a supportive, accommodating associate professor or full professor to do in giving an assistant professor advice about her research. You may want to rethink this—those kinds of statements. I responded in a very cordial way and explained that, it's not gonna happen, we ended up with over three hundred responses. We're interested in the aggregate data. We're not at all interested in individual responses nor are we gonna be looking through this data in ways to try to figure out who people are, that's not the point of this project....A lot of female professors that I'm acquainted with, even in associate and full rank, came up to me and said, wow, I found your survey really interesting, I'm glad you're doing this research, this is really cool, I'm excited to see what you find. And yet I got these two unsupportive, cynical, not helpful emails from these men that I didn't even personally know.

The two men who emailed Lisa did so assuming her incompetence, that she could not possibly understand that her survey was flawed in the ways they were pointing out. And rather than writing to her in a way that was collegial, they wrote to her and mansplained her own research project to her. As Manne explains about epistemic entitlement, the position the mansplainers put Lisa into was one in which she had little choice but to respond politely and assure them that she was not interested in identifying individual survey responders; Lisa's responses were calm and academic, not at all pointed in the ways the men's emails to her were. Had she responded in kind, she may have been "in danger of humiliating" them (Manne, *Entitled* 143). On the other hand, Lisa's female colleagues could easily see the value of her research and told her as much; they were not, we might say, burdened by the belief that Lisa was incompetent in her own field of study.

The "rules of the game" when it comes to negotiating for salary and raises came up in two stories that highlight the ways women in English departments feel the need to advocate for themselves in ways they do not see men having to do. Men, it seems, are automatically offered the higher salary and the higher raise, as they are understood to be entitled to more money. Alexandra, an assistant professor at a regional university, was hired at the same time as a male colleague.

> They offered me the job, and they said, this is the salary, and I said, okay, great. I need a couple days to reach out to the other people I've interviewed with and then I will shoot you back an email with a counteroffer. I did that. I didn't tell them this is the job I want. I wanted a couple days to look through their tables and make a good counteroffer. And so I countered and we did the normal thing

where they meet me halfway and we're all good. I found out later from somebody else on the search committee that after we negotiated, when they offered the job to my male counterpart, they just offered him what I had negotiated for.

Alexandra did the work of negotiating—of researching, of coming back with a counteroffer—and her male colleague benefits from her labor without even knowing about it.

And I was pissed, I'll be honest with you. And they said, "He was right out of graduate school." I was like, "I don't give a shit." He doesn't know how to play the game? So he gets to benefit from me. And when you do a counteroffer, it's a risk because they could have said, "Who do you think you are by asking for X more dollars per year? We're gonna rescind our offer." It's a risk making a counteroffer. I could admit that I felt comfortable making a counter because I already had a tenure-track job and blah blah blah. I was still just like, "You don't just offer him…" They're like, "Well, he had a family." Right? And so I had this moment of like, this to me is exactly what is wrong. Also, you guys never should have told me this. The person who told me this was telling me this in the guise of, isn't it great you work for such a good and caring work environment.

That her coworker believed Alexandra would be *pleased* by this information suggests nothing more than that person's utter cluelessness. The only way to interpret this situation as reflecting a caring work environment is to see men as in need of extra care when it comes to negotiating salary.

This guy doesn't know any of this. If he does, he's never said anything. So I work with this person and there are moments when I'm sitting across from him in a meeting and I'm thinking, you got that extra couple thousand dollars because of me. And that's not fair to him… That is what is wrong with higher ed right now. As a woman, I take this risk, I do this work, I do this research about how to do the job market, I contact my mentors, I do all this and he just walks in and they're like, here you go. I found that really insulting. I know that happens all the time….I'll also point out that he came right out of grad school and I had four years of experience. I was a WPA at my last job. You hired me because you wanted me to be WPA. You gave this guy the same amount of money even though he doesn't have the same experience.

Not only does her male colleague receive the benefit of Alexandra's negotiating skills, but he earns the same salary as she does despite her having four years' experience on him. Alexandra is not being rewarded for her negotiating skills or for her years of experience, both of which make her an asset to her department. Her male colleague benefits from her work without his even knowing about it.

Theresa, a full professor at a public university, tells me story that similarly highlights the ways women are expected to do more work than men in order to get their due. Women must know the rules of the game in ways that men need not, as those in power will simply grant men the salary and raises they believe they are entitled to.

> When I was coming up for full, I had a male colleague who was coming up for associate at the same time. We're friendly. I found out that his raise and my raise, the percentage was vastly different. Mine was the university sanctioned 10% and his was 17% and that was horrifying and made me want to quit and I just couldn't understand. My chair's response was, I can't talk about other people's situations. That's private information. My response to that was to go check out from the library the green book that has everybody's salaries. I wrote down every single person. I put together a chart. In order to get any kind of salary equity raise—and there was a gender salary equity study going on—you have to do all the work. I did all of that, and I was like, this is not fair at all. So I was able to advocate for myself, but I was just so pissed off. But even if he went on the market and he had another offer, why wouldn't you give that same advice to someone else? That's one of the things that I see really happening: unless there's someone who's an advocate for you and tells you along the way, whether you're male or female, here's how you play the game, that's part of what I don't see happening. I don't see transparency in that, and I wish there was more.

Like Alexandra, Theresa finds herself with direct knowledge about the salary of a male colleague that exposes the ways she is not being treated equitably. Theresa had to do extra labor to demonstrate to her chair that her male colleague's salary situation was not, in fact, private, as they were at a public institution. So she collected the information she needed to collect in order to get the raise she was entitled to, but she had no help in doing so. She needed to already know how to play the game; there was nobody there to help her or to advocate for her. If she hadn't learned about her colleague's 17% raise to her 10% raise, she would not have been able to advocate for herself.

Both Alexandra and Theresa are on the tenure track; life is harder, as we know, for those not on the tenure track. Monica, a lecturer at a research-1 university, tells me a story about being passed over again and again for a leadership position only to see the jobs go to white men in the department.

I applied to be part of the leadership at least twice, actually three times. Once they were late to my interview. They showed up late—oh, we're coming from lunch. So you really respect me. I get that. So then I was thrown off the whole interview. They asked me a question that I did not have the answer to and they're like, no, keep trying, and I was like, I didn't do research on that question, so I don't have an answer, but I have answers to lots of other ones if you would ask them. And the man who wears sweatpants got the job that year.

Monica had told me earlier in the interview about the differences she notices in terms of how people dress: the more likely they are to be a leader, the more likely they are to dress down. "I have worked with many men who come in in cut-off jean shorts and ratty t-shirts and there's one who briefly was part of the leadership who comes in every day in sweatpants and a t-shirt and he wears a flannel or something and a blazer over it." She continues her story:

And then this past year I applied again and it was to be the coordinator for a class that I teach a lot—I teach it every semester—and I'm very, very knowledgeable about what the students need, how the class works, what the students' lives are like, and again, the job went to an older white man. Their reason was, he has more experience, and I'm just like, but I know the class. Nobody knows that class like I do. I pretty much was the perfect candidate for it and didn't get the job.

Monica tells me, too, that her male colleagues cannot seem to get past the fact that she has what she calls a "baby face" and that this seems to cause them to "treat me paternalistically where they want to give me advice about everything. They expect me to listen to all their advice because they have all the knowledge." Yet when it came to the coordinator position that she did not get, the man who *did* get it ended up coming to her for advice because, as she said, she knows the class really well.

Now I'm supposed to help the man they actually picked. I'm supposed to help him because he doesn't know the class as well, and he's asking people who taught the class for advice because he hasn't taught it in years. We've restructured the class since he taught it. It's so infuriating. It's a specific set of students who would take that class and being someone who has worked with that specific subset of students, I know everything they're freaking out about, I know all the reasons to tell them to take this particular class, and he's just like, well, what about advice about this? I'm like, sure, let me give you some advice.

We can hear the frustration in these women's voices. They are pissed. They are horrified. They are infuriated. Experiencing misogyny in the course of their work lives in English departments makes women angry, and anger is not an emotion that we associate with women who conform to the gender roles patriarchy has prescribed for them. As I noted in the Introduction, many of the women who spoke with me overcame whatever fears they may have had about being labeled a gossip, about being considered ungrateful for their job, or about the possibility of retaliation by pointing to the power of storytelling and the need to build a collective. It is only now, in thinking about these stories again in this context, that I see the way these women's anger surfaces in ways that demonstrate not just their commitment to one another and to women's storytelling but also to confronting change in that storytelling. As Soraya Chemaly writes in *Rage Becomes Her*, "Anger remains the emotion that is least acceptable for girls and women because it is the first line of defense against injustice. Believing that you have the *right* to use your anger with power reflects multiple, overlapping social entitlements" (24). I can't say to what extent the women I interviewed expressed their anger *at the time*, but that they were able to express their anger with me tells me that they experienced a sense of entitlement in the process of telling their stories. Of course, it is true that Alexandra, Theresa, and Monica were not expressing anger *at me*, their interlocutor, but instead at third parties who were not present during our conversations, so their expressions of anger did not carry the same risk as a direct expression might. And we see, with Lisa's story, that she did not respond with anger but rather with cordiality to the men who questioned her competence with respect to her research project. Had she responded with anger—as she had every right to do—she would likely have been punished with another of what Manne calls down-girl moves.

Putting Women in Their Place

Of course, Lisa *was* punished with down-girl moves; she was belittled and she was mansplained to. Recall that Manne writes that

> Girls and women may be down-ranked or deprived relative to more or less anything that people typically value—material goods, social status, moral reputation, and intellectual credentials, among other realms of human achievement, esteem, pride, and so on. This may happen in numerous ways: condescending, mansplaining, moralizing, blaming, punishing, silencing, lampooning, satirizing,

sexualizing, belittling, caricaturizing, exploiting, erasing, and evincing pointed indifference. (*Down Girl* 30)

Several women told me stories about being down-ranked or punished after in some way seeking masculine-coded goods. These punishments range from being insulted to being ignored to being yelled at to being passed over for promotion to being threatened.

Amanda, a third-year doctoral student at a Research-2 university, tells me that she was punished in a couple ways after expressing anger at the ways she was being treated by faculty in her program.

> In my second year here, I had pretty much decided that I wasn't taking any more crap from my faculty members who were not treating me well and not giving me the same opportunities as my colleagues, and I'll admit that I was often quite angry and my male colleagues told me that nobody would work with me because rather than being understanding and easygoing and willing to let faculty do whatever they wanted and treat me poorly, instead, I was angry. I was standing up for myself, I was seeking ways to maybe try to change things, and I just got put way back in my place right away. It was verbalized that nobody would work with me.

Amanda's expression of anger—an outlaw emotion, according to Alison Jaggar—positioned her as somebody who understood herself to have *entitlements* to respect, and that situation only continued to lead to more punishments for her.

> I am not doing a creative dissertation and I am only working with one creative writing faculty member because I can't work with the other ones. And this plays out in the ways we get responses on our work—whether it's not getting any— which happened to me. For a full year I got no written feedback on my work—or it's the social interactions or even things like, another male grad student and I were going to miss the same week of class, both for professional events, and I was given extensive makeup work and he was given none. Things like that. And it becomes a situation of death by a thousand cuts.

When women step out of line, so to speak, by claiming entitlement to anger, by claiming to know, by claiming access to any masculine-coded good, they are often, as Amanda says, put back in their place. Where is that place that women belong? A place of quiet acquiescence, a place of no complaining, a place of acceptance of any and all vitriol that comes your way. A place in which you accept that it is your job to give and not to take.

Lucy, a lecturer at a liberal arts college, describes the ways she's been put back in her place with her WPA:

> I feel like right now I'm actually being punished for standing up for myself and, um, if I cry, I'm sorry. My WPA is—I feel like I'm in an abusive relationship. I feel like...I feel like I'm the wife in this situation and she's the husband. When I stroke her ego and play along, we have a little bit of a honeymoon period, but any time I want to be in charge or be assertive, then I'm punished.

When I ask Lucy how she's punished, she says, "Well, whenever I try to be assertive or have an opinion about something, if it runs any kind of contrary to hers, she gets upset and then she'll tell me things like, 'Oh, that's not your place to say,' or 'That's really smart even though you only have a master's degree.'"

Laura echoes Lucy's remark about women who are assertive, noting that women who try to be assertive are immediately marked.

> I think we're punished by ironically many of the same means that we are expected to perform. One way is when women are assertive, when women are taking control over what they deserve as graduate students, as members of any academic community, it's very easy to mark those women as—I'm trying to think of specific phrases that have been used about me. I pride myself on being someone who's kind and who tries my best to lift people up, and that's a lot of feminine labor, but I know that word has gotten around about me being very aggressive and mean and rude and I have been tattled on to the graduate director.

Sara tells me that she has witnessed a colleague be punished for straying from her place of acquiescence and care:

> I actually think a female faculty member here who I'm good friends with has experienced this over and over. She is on record the only faculty member in this whole college who did not receive her promotion with two well received books out and she has to go up again. I'm convinced it's because she does not behave, she's not warm and fuzzy. She's friendly, but she's direct and critical and I think people perceive that as inappropriate but her male colleague right next to her can do that and nobody says a word. She's a prime example and she's constantly hurt—and of course, it just makes her more critical.

When Rebecca, an associate professor at a public liberal arts college, objected to her chair's decision about a search committee, she, too, was put in her place.

We have a search coming up and the provost decided that our field was too narrow because it was only British literature and it was an open field, so my department basically said, oh, no problem, we're more than happy to do a search that attracts up to a thousand applicants, and I said, that's absolutely ridiculous. We really need to step back and say, as experts in the field, we know what the job market looks like and there are reasons why we set the parameters as wide or as narrow as we decided. What happened then is that several of my colleagues actually started yelling at me because I was attacking the chair who wasn't stepping up for us versus saying, oh, I think you might be right. Maybe we can change that. So it's that kind of pattern. When a woman says, oh we can't do that, usually the reaction is, step down, don't freak out, just calm down, and when a man says it, the chair will actually go and advocate for that change.

A woman's place is one to which she can be returned by way of yelling, by way of being marked as aggressive or assertive, by way of being insulted. Alexandra tells me a story about a colleague who tried to put her back in her place after a department meeting discussion:

In the last department meeting, we had this heated discussion about textbooks, which, you know—textbooks—and we had a faculty member say something and I raised my hand and I said, I don't know that that's fair to this, and it was a woman I was having this conversation with, and she shot back and I shot back a little bit, and then after the meeting, one of my male colleagues came up to me and said, you know, you don't have tenure yet. I was like, I know. I'm aware of my positionality. I feel like—the charitable side of me was like, he was just trying to be nice, but this other side of me was like, dude, I got this. I'm aware. I went and talked to the woman after the meeting, and she was totally cool with it. She's a pretty assertive woman and so she was not threatened by that, and I'm like, so this man viewed two women having a heated discussion and felt the need to warn me, and I was like, I can manage my own relationships with faculty members, thank you.

Her male colleague wasn't even the one she was having the discussion with, but he felt the need to protect her from potentially being put in her place by the woman she *was* in conversation with. So he put her in her place.

A woman in her place is also "out of line," as Patricia, an associate professor at an HBCU, explains:

We have a civility clause in our contract, and it's part of our tenure review, and any time that we step out of line we are threatened with being uncivil. I have never heard of a man being accused of being uncivil, but several of my female colleagues and I have been verbally threatened with it and one woman has been written up several times because she calls her chairperson on straight up lying. I'm at the point where, I was offered the first person position on a grant and somebody else walked into the grant, and I said I'd rather share the credit than cause the inevitable fallout of standing up for my rights to be the first person on it because it'll be ten years down the road, you need to take a stance on whose side you are on, kind of deal.

In Patricia's case, we see that calling someone out for lying and standing up for your rights are both considered to be moves that would be "out of line" for a woman in her department. And standing up for your rights comes with an "inevitable fallout."

If we take all of these stories together, we can see that when she is in her place, a woman is also in line, and when either or both of these is true, a woman is not aggressive or angry or assertive. She does not have opinions. She does not ask for feedback on her work if she is a student. She does not attempt to make suggestions about her area of academic expertise. She does not call out anybody in her department, most especially her chairperson, for lying. She does not take credit for her work. She does not try to change things.

She certainly does not try to establish boundaries. Two women I spoke with told me stories about trying to establish boundaries between their personal and professional lives, with varying degrees of success. First is Molly, an assistant professor and Writing Program Administrator (WPA) at a Hispanic-serving institution, who included a policy on her syllabus saying that if her office door is closed, "then you should consider it as if I'm not there and you should come back later or should send me an email or you should wait until you see me in class because the door is shut for a reason. I put it there mainly because these boundaries are super important for my own sanity." Before she had written this policy into her syllabus, when she was in her office on campus with the door closed, "I had noticed that, when I was on campus, I was in my office, but I had the door closed, and it was not my office hours, I was trying to concentrate, even if I'm on the phone, even if I'm in a meeting with other people, that students would consistently be knocking on the door or trying to get my attention—the way our offices are set up, there's this window shade, but you can see right through it, they can see that I'm here." At Molly's first retention meeting, the only policy from her syllabus that was brought up was this one. One of the male members of the retention committee didn't understand it, so asked for an explanation.

> I said, I consider myself to be an ally for my students, I'm someone that they feel comfortable approaching, but I can't be there twelve hours a day at their disposal. It's not healthy for me as an individual to be consistently asked for something by students or colleagues.

Molly's explanation was "brushed away as if my explanation wasn't sufficient," and she left the meeting with the sense that "When I try to set these boundaries for myself, it's almost seen as, you don't care about your students. I care about my students very much; I also care about myself and resisting that burnout especially near the end of the semester." Though she questioned the inclusion of the policy on her syllabus, she ultimately kept it in, telling students in class, "I'm an introvert, I need to be able to recharge after I teach a class, I need those fifteen minutes and if I have you or anyone else knocking on my door, it's really disruptive to my process of recharging, and for the most part, my students are like, okay, it's not a big deal." Molly had no trouble establishing boundaries with her students, but when an administrator saw the policy on her syllabus, he objected.

Even more egregious than Molly's story in terms of not being able to establish boundaries is Patricia's story of what happened to her when she returned from maternity leave.

> I breastfed, so I had to have some time to pump, and at first, I had a very discrete sign on my door that said, "Please do not disturb." Well, people would still knock on my door and the secretary who's across the hall would say, "She's in there, keep knocking." So then I had a happy little cartoon cow that said, "I'm making food for my baby. Come back later," and she would still send people and say, "She's in there, keep knocking." So I finally put a picture that said, "I am breastfeeding and I don't have clothes on. Come back later." And I got yelled at for an inappropriate sign on my door. Yes, we have private offices, but people were battering my door and being encouraged by other people in my department instead of, "Hey, she may need a minute."

In her place, a woman may not be alone. In her place and in line, a woman is meant to be giving her care and attention to others, not to herself. She is not meant to be "recharging," as Molly was with her office door closed. She is not meant to be attending to her own family's needs, as Patricia was as she pumped breast milk for her baby. In settings like English departments where we see some feminist progress, Manne explains that

> When demand for her attention exceeds supply on a grand scale, it is not surprising to find practices of men trying to turn the heads of women previously unknown to them—via catcalling and wolf-whistling and various forms of online trolling (from the patently abusive to ostensibly reasonable demands for rational debate, which unfortunately sometimes result in her being belittled, insulted, or mansplained to). In public settings, she is told to smile or asked what she's thinking by many a (male) stranger—especially when she appears to be "deep inside her own head" or "off in her own little world," i.e., appearing to think her own thoughts, her attention inwardly, rather than outwardly, focused. These gestures are then supposed to either *make her look*, or else force her to stonewall—a withholding, rather than sheer absence, of reaction. So her silence is icy; her neutral expression, sullen. Her not looking is snubbing; her passivity, aggression. (*Down Girl* 176)

When she is not freely giving her attention—when the supply is lower than the demand—others will demand it in ways that *make her look* and destroy her ability to concentrate. When Molly explained to her students that she needed them to stop making her look, they seemed to understand. When Patricia tried again and again to articulate her need for privacy via signs on her door, interrupters were continuously encouraged to keep knocking until she made a sign that was "inappropriate." And she was, of course, punished by being yelled at.

Patriarchy's norms position women as givers and men as takers; women give attention, affection, care, loyalty, and nurturance, while men take respect, authority, leadership, competitive advantage, and are protected from negative feelings like shame and humiliation. Misogyny targets those women who try to take those masculine-coded goods for themselves, and women know that they are not supposed to demonstrate characteristics that are typically identified as masculine. Jeanne, a second-year doctoral student at a Research-2 university, wonders aloud why she found herself the object of a male colleague's silent treatment. "There have to be markers that make someone a target. I do think some of it's my…it's hard to talk about myself and not sound like I'm being egotistical. I'm confident and I think that can mark you because it's coded masculine." Anna, too, understands that women are not supposed to be confident: "I know some women in the program, if they are particularly competitive, that is seen as not being a good quality as if being proud of your accomplishments is something that you should not do as a woman, and I haven't noticed that with a lot of men in the program." Confident, proud women are less likely to direct their attention to men simply because men ask for it, and they are much harder to put in their place. In fact, their place may be an entirely different one than patriarchy has carved out for them. Or it can be, eventually.

Confident women are less likely to *give* what is not deserved. Here's Laura again, telling a story about a male graduate student colleague:

> We were at an end-of-semester thing after my first year and we were at a bar and we'd been drinking a lot and he looked at me and he was like, "I want to tell you something," and I was like, "Yes, what is it?" and he was like, "You know, I don't think many people are smarter than me. I have met very few people who I think are smarter, but I realize after this first year that you actually are." And I felt this moment, this bubbling up to give that female energy. To do the labor of telling him, "Oh no, don't worry, you're just as smart." Or, "Maybe I just talk more in class than you" or something like that, but instead I said, "Thank you" and we sat there in silence. I think that was the first instance where I felt like I was not going to apologize because I am smarter than him. I'm way smarter than him. He doesn't even try.

Do I even need to comment on the male graduate student saying that he's met very few people he thinks are smarter than him? On the alleged compliment he delivers to Laura that is actually a request for affirmation? What strikes me as far more important to remark on is Laura's refusal to offer him that affirmation, to engage in that emotional labor. It may seem small, but it is a remarkable achievement, one that disrupts the received narrative in which the woman comforts the man when his ego is damaged. Laura refuses to play her part in the narrative patriarchy has constructed and, as a result, the story is stymied. They sit there in silence. When I tell Laura that I'm shocked at how blatant the ask was here, she responds, "It's kind of lonely sitting in that silence, though."

Though it may be lonely sitting in that silence, my guess is that Laura's telling of this story will ring true for many readers, that those readers may have stories of their own to share, and that that silence will be drowned out by more storytelling. This is the point of my telling them here: to encourage more telling, to drown out the lonely silence that comes from disrupting patriarchy, to make stories like Laura's—like all of the interviewees'—more common and thus more a part of our narrative habitus. I want these stories to become our go-to stories, the ones we reach for when we talk about patriarchy and misogyny in academia generally and English departments specifically. I want us to stop pretending that we work in egalitarian spaces.

References

Chemaly, Soraya. *Rage Becomes Her.* New York: Atria Books, 2018.
Manne, Kate. *Down Girl: The Logic of Misogyny.* New York: Oxford UP, 2018.
———. *Entitled: How Male Privilege Hurts Women.* New York: Crown, 2020.
Vettese, Troy. "Sexism in the Academy." *n+1* 34 (2019).

4

Sexual Harassment and Women's Credibility

I believe, in fact, that the slur *slut* carries within it, Trojan-horse style, silence as its true intent. That the opposite of *slut* is not virtue but voice.

—Lacy Crawford, *Notes on a Silencing*

There's no way I'm saying anything to you that's surprising.

—Erika, Professor

Susan, an assistant professor at a four-year college that was, until five years ago, a community college, tells me a story about being asked by her department head to mentor two new hires in online teaching. Part of that mentoring involved meeting with the two new faculty members in their offices during office hours, "doing a lot of, here's how you teach online, best practices of teaching online, etc." Not long after she had begun this work, Susan learned that one of the women in her department "emailed several of the VPs and the department head and said that I was being inappropriately affectionate with both of these new hires and they felt like I was—" Susan stops talking here. She pauses. She doesn't know how to finish her sentence.

> The head of the department cc'ed me on his answer and said, "I've never gotten that vibe from Susan before, but what do you mean by inappropriately affectionate," and then she replied that I was sitting in their office hours and I was talking to them for longer than twenty minutes and I was like, yeah, because we're going over best practices of how to teach online. I'm sorry I can't do that in twenty minutes! And that I seem to be contacting them a lot and I seem to know a lot about them—and I'm like, yes, because I talk to them! Then I was asked to make sure that if I was ever talking to one of the new hires, that we had to be meeting in the hallway. Are we adults?

Susan pauses again before continuing.

> We had to be in the hallway, and I was never allowed into their offices—so then I moved our meetings online. This is ridiculous. What am I, 12? Then I had a very stern email from the head of our department, who is again, 29, who said, you want to avoid any appearances that you're grooming these two new hires. Grooming them? Into what? Better online teachers? I emailed back and said, "Isn't the English language interesting, how words can have multiple meanings? I don't appreciate your use of the word *grooming* as if I'm a sexual predator." He emailed back and pretty much said, you're right, poor choice of words, but you do need to avoid any appearance of sexual misconduct.

Here we have a woman defying gender norms, exhibiting power over two new male faculty members as she trains them in the best practices of online teaching, and another woman in the department tries to shock her back into place by accusing her of being sexually inappropriate with her colleagues. Susan's colleague establishes a random norm—twenty minutes—to which Susan is unable to conform and thus, Susan is subject to misogynistic punishment. The punishment in this case is particularly egregious given that it comes in the form of an accusation of sexual misconduct, the very complaint so many women in academia make that is not heard, that is not believed. Even when Susan calls her department head out on his misogynistic behavior, he doubles down and reminds her to "avoid any appearance of sexual misconduct," ignoring the fact that there was never any appearance of such in the first place.

Susan's story shows us that doubting women is ideologically a given; as Leigh Gilmore writes in *Tainted Witness*, "Doubting women is enshrined in the law, represented in literature, repeated in culture, embedded in institutions, and associated with benefits like rationality and objectivity. Quite simply, women encounter doubt as a condition of bearing witness" (19–20). And women are persuaded to doubt themselves, wondering if what has happened to them has really happened, wondering if they should say out loud what they want or need to say. In her essay, "The Cost of Disbelieving," Jaclyn Friedman writes, "I know of no woman who doesn't house inside her the nagging feeling that maybe what she has to say is not that important, or will cause too much trouble, or put her in danger. I know of no woman who has not at least some of the time allowed that feeling to prevail, to smother her impulse to speak" (303). Just as women are not the cultural bearers of intellectual authority, leadership or respect, as we saw in Chapter 3, women are not the cultural bearers of credibility. And, as Friedman points out, "social researchers have long demonstrated that it's not just that we hold women to much higher standards than we do men before we believe them. It's more perverse than that: we *prefer* not finding women credible." Friedman continues:

> As a culture, we hate to believe women, and we penalize them for forcing us to do so. In other words, as women's credibility increases, especially in ways that defy gender norms, their social likability decreases. They become shrill bitches, ball busters, too aggressive, too bossy, such intolerable know-it-alls. It is not enough that we demand women clear a much higher bar than men to do prove their trustworthiness. We're mad when they manage to succeed anyway. And we're all paying the price for that anger. (303)

As I noted in the Introduction, there are a few scholars in the field talking about sexual harassment in English Studies; Patricia Freitag Ericsson's edited collection, *Sexual Harassment and Cultural Change in Writing Studies*, provides a variety of helpful definitions of and scenarios for talking about sexual harassment, while Laura Micciche's 2018 Where We Are section of *Composition Studies* focused on #MeToo and academia provides a handful of stories from women with the least power in rhetoric and composition. In this chapter, I provide more stories, more women talking about the experience so many women have had in their workplaces, in an effort to disabuse us of the belief that we are somehow above the fray when it comes to sexual harassment. We are not. It happens. Nobody talks about it.

We can understand why nobody talks about it. As Gilmore explains, "Shaming, victim blaming, discrediting, and denunciation attach to women's testimony so predictably, and are so regularly associated with it, that these negative affects function as prolepsis: they are a threat that prevents women from testifying" (7). Kelly, a professor at a public university, tells me that when it comes to sexual harassment in her department, "the idea of actually speaking up about these things or suggesting that there's—making mention of investigations, that kind of thing, is somehow harassment." This, Kelly makes clear to me, is said by men in the department, and it has "led to some thorny ethical problems." Similarly, Moira, an associate professor at a Research-1 university, tells me that she's not in a department

> where someone is going to leer at my breasts.... I would say that the majority of the men and women of all races and ethnicities would consider themselves self-aware, the sort of people who get the sexual harassment training every year and think, "Oh god, this again. I study the way culture is made. I study literature. I study cultural theory, so this doesn't really apply to me."

In Kelly's department, they don't talk about it because that would be considered a form of harassment in itself, and in Moira's department, their alleged awareness of how sexual harassment works somehow precludes their actually perpetrating it.

The women who spoke with me about their experiences with misogyny in English departments knew they would not be shamed or blamed for what they told me, and they knew their stories would remain confidential. They knew they would be believed. And so they broke their silence.

Witnessing Colleagues' Harassment of Others

Several women I spoke with told me stories about their knowledge of colleagues who harass others, particularly male professors' harassment of graduate and undergraduate students. Eva, a first-year doctoral student at a state university, tells me, "In every English program I've been in, I have had to deal with professors hitting on students or having children with students and that's devastating to me." Later in our conversation, Eva tells me about a situation when she was an undergraduate student:

> I had a faculty member that I reported for trying to have an affair with one of my friends when I was an undergrad and he came up to me after it happened at a coffee shop and he said, "I just want you to know, I'm sorry," and I was like, fuck you, you shouldn't have to apologize in the first place. You shouldn't have done that. You shouldn't have made me trust you and then devastate me. He wasn't removed from his position. He wasn't demoted. He didn't have to face any consequences for hitting on a student and telling her he wanted to touch her ass.

Meg, an instructor at a Research-1 university, tells me, "Male professors just in general having flirtatious and romantic relationships with graduate students is a thing that I've seen in my department and just growing up in academia and I think that that has colored the dynamic between male professors and female graduate students in ways that are uncomfortable." Amanda, a third year doctoral student at a Research-2 university, tells me, "I know first- or second-hand of several male faculty members in my department who have made moves on graduate students and seem to expect that grad students will give them that kind of relationship or favors, however you want to put it, probably depends on the person, but I couldn't tell you a single female faculty member who has done that to a graduate student in my department."

Monica, an instructor at a large public university, reiterates the silencing that happens around such issues:

> Nobody really comes out and says that kind of thing, but we had a man who was an adjunct for many, many years, and he also worked for tutoring…and the people who did the scheduling for that tutoring told me that he was never to be assigned a female student and that everyone kinda had this sense about him, but it took years for him to be fired.

We saw this kind of silencing in the work that Micciche published in *Composition Studies*; as editor of that Where We Are section, Micciche noted that stories of serial harassers are "passed discreetly among friends at conferences and in hallways" rather than openly talked about. Later in her conversation with me, Meg noted this backchannel means of sharing information, too.

> In general, I would say the sexual and flirtatious dynamics that play out at departmental events and of course conferences, but even at the departmental level, where just like people go out and drink together and end up having physical interactions and then you go back and, I don't know, I think it just creates dynamics…. Another part of it is that it's clandestine, it's these things that you have to find out through this backchannel of talk between women primarily where we just tell each other. So, for example, the person who was found guilty of sexual harassment—after sort of a year-long investigation, the way that people prevent him from having female mentees is just this backchannel.

Women protect one another by sharing stories of men behaving badly; they protect female students by talking with one another backchannel. And they self-shame when they find themselves unable to interrupt harassment in the moment. Here's Marie, an instructor at a Research-1 university:

> I can think of this one joke that this faculty member said to someone else—it had to do with something she did the night before—that was the punchline. I remember being shocked, but then also later when I went to talk to her, being angry that I didn't say something in the moment. I was like, "Why didn't you speak up? Why didn't you say, 'That's completely unacceptable'?" Then there was my own sort of self-shame for not saying anything and then having to see this person in the hallway and think, "You're an asshole."

And when women do say something, they are—unsurprisingly—challenged on their interpretation of the situation. Here's Pam, a professor and chair at a Research-1 university:

> Our former chair groped his colleague under the table twice and she went to the OEO (Office of Equal Opportunity), and he asked her, how were you dressed and why did it take so long to report? And then he asked everyone sitting at the table—they were all men—did you see anything inappropriate, and they all said no because they couldn't see the groping under the table.... I had gone to the dean to tell what happened and he looked at me and said, "Oh, this is all just he said/she said. These are just allegations." And I did not know that he had interviewed the former chair to be the new associate dean and so he gave him the position anyway. So you just keep getting promoted anyway if you're a guy. It doesn't matter. I almost think they enjoy it—seeing other guys get away with it.

Pam was told that her concerns about sexual harassment were just gossip, a means of dismissal I referenced in the Introduction when I wrote that many women who spoke with me recognized that they may be punished for speaking about their experiences with misogyny by being characterized as a gossip. Sarah Deer and Bonnie Clairmont note, too, that "The English word *gossip*, with its negative connotations, is often used in an attempt to undermine women who seek to share information about dangerous men" (15). They propose that we "stop calling it *gossip* and start calling it *truth-telling*" (16).

One of the most devastating stories I heard from an interviewee about the sexual misconduct of a colleague comes from Jody, a department chair at a community college. She told me first about the effects of the situation. A female colleague "sought to undermine and bully me at every single juncture—publicly." When Jody first took over as department chair, this colleague "decided that it was appropriate to bully me in front of the department at countless department meetings. Department meeting after department meeting, it would be antagonism, it was behind-the-scenes text messaging. I was called a mole for administration." Jody tells me, "It was just relentless."

> I got a nasty email every day for the first six weeks on the job. Every single day. I got from somebody in the department something—some sort of complaint, some sort of snarkiness, some sort of—to the point where we were in a meeting and a faculty member said, "I was gonna say something at the department meeting, but I didn't want that faculty member to turn on me the way she has on you."

The bullying got so extreme that Jody considered quitting, "every single day, for a year and a half. Every single day I was gonna quit." Later in the interview, Jody tells me that the reason this female colleague was so upset with her was that she, Jody, had reported a Title IX violation against one of their male colleagues.

> He was fired, he committed suicide, and she held me partly responsible. If you were to ask her, is this what happened, I don't think she would say that's what happened. I think she would say, Jody is just a terrible boss. She would say that I'm dictatorial and draconian and not willing to listen, and she would say, of course I wouldn't want a student abused, and she was mad about how it was all handled.

Jody tells me that the reporting was handled badly, that when she first reported it, it wasn't followed up. "I had to escalate it. I know that they say you can't fire whistleblowers…but I make a thousand decisions a day—any one of those, someone could say, that was the wrong one, and you deserve to be fired. So I knew when I escalated the report, there could be consequences and I did it anyway and I have to live with the consequences of it. It's just awful. It was awful for everybody." There had never been any question of whether the male colleague had committed the act; it was documented and there was evidence. And when a student came to Jody to report the sexual misconduct, Jody reported it to Title IX.

> For me, it was emotionally gut-wrenching. This was a colleague that I liked, it was a student that I liked. People didn't want to believe that it happened, I didn't want to believe that it happened, but it did, there was documentation and evidence of it. I still feel tremendous—I don't feel so much guilt about it anymore. I feel the burden of the weight of the experience. It changed me. I had a breakdown at work. I felt I was the scapegoat for people's anger at the whole situation. He was very well liked and I wish that it had been different.

It was hard to hear Jody's story because I could still hear the pain in her voice as she told it. In her situation, talking about it, doing her job, reporting a Title IX violation, cost her so very much emotionally. The abuse came primarily from one female colleague, and Jody eventually began to question the extent to which she deserved the bullying.

> It's hard to get outside of myself in this experience and maybe that's what bullying is supposed to do—it's supposed to make you internalize it. Kids who are bullied don't go, well this is a very common experience for every fifteen-year-old. No.

They go, everybody hates me. What did I do to deserve this? It's hard for me to step out of this and see it as not personal.

In this situation, it's not just that Jody's story was doubted; rather, Jody's response was acted on in ways she never could have anticipated and she was held responsible for the actions of the sexual abuser who decided to take his own life. The reporting of one form of misogyny—sexual abuse—led to further misogyny when Jody diverged from the gender norm of staying quiet about the misconduct of men. Manne calls "himpathy" "the disproportionate or inappropriate sympathy extended to a male perpetrator over his similarly or less privileged female targets or victims, in cases of sexual assault, harassment, and other misogynistic behavior" (*Entitled* 36). Jody emphasizes in her story that nobody wanted to believe that their male colleague could have done this terrible thing: "Of course he didn't do this, everybody loves him, the student must be lying, how can you believe the student?" And, as if in response to Jody's exact situation, Manne explains, "Himpathy goes hand in hand with blaming or erasing the targets of misogyny. When the sympathetic focus is on the perpetrator, she will often be subject to suspicion and aggression for drawing attention to his misdeeds" (*Entitled* 37). Rather than hold the male colleague accountable for his own actions, Jody's colleagues held her—the one who told—accountable for his actions. She is blamed and shamed; he is absolved as the sympathy flows in his direction. And Jody is left to pick up the pieces as she works for literally years to process what has happened to her.

I followed up with Jody in the early spring of 2022, and she told me that our interview in 2019 was one of the galvanizing forces for her decision to go back to the slew of emails she had in her inbox outlining the complicity of the college's provost in ignoring the sexual misconduct situation between the faculty member and the student. While Jody was busy feeling guilty about having reported the faculty member to Title IX and her colleague was busy bullying her in retaliation for said reporting, Jody tells me that it took her a good year before she was able to go back to her emails and read what was right there in front of her: the provost had told her to "back off, that the student was lying, that she had mental health issues." Jody explains:

> He let the bullying happen because if the target was on me, it wasn't on him and his complicity in it. That took me about a year to figure out. I couldn't understand, why was I being targeted so badly at this school? I reported a faculty member who was doing terrible things, and why was it being accepted? I think part of

it was they wanted me to go, but also I think if people knew more about it, they would see his [the provost's] part in it. But if the focus was on me, it wasn't on him. It took me a long time to see that. My guilt about the whole thing kept me kind of isolated.

The provost has since left the college and Jody has been promoted to a dean position. The situation has left its mark, however. "Now I'm considered the person that will tattle. People will say, you have to be careful around me because I'm the person who will go to HR with a complaint." But then there's also this: "Now, I'm fearless at work. I'm like, what are you gonna do? The worst has already happened. I'm on the other side of it. The collateral damage was so extensive. It just has this ripple effect, sending shockwaves through people's lives."

Experiencing Sexual Harassment at School and Work

In contrast to Jody's detailed story about reporting a colleague for sexual misconduct, Bonnie, a professor at a Research-2 university, tells me, "I don't want to go into great detail about graduate school, but…I guess sexual harassment is a form of misogyny?" She told me nothing else after I said that yes, sexual harassment is a form of misogyny. The norm of remaining silent about sexual harassment remained in place in Bonnie's case, despite the fact that she responded to a request for an interview about misogyny in English departments. This is not a criticism of Bonnie; this is, instead, a remark on how powerfully that norm acts on us.

Graduate students told me a number of stories about feeling unsafe sexually in their departments, in the presence of both male graduate students and male faculty. Caroline, a third-year doctoral student at a Research-2 university, tells me

> I feel very vulnerable and unsafe sexually, too.…I'm still struggling to figure out how I should go about this—whether I should report this or talking to someone about ethics…about sexist things—how much is it considered sexual harassment? To me, if it was making me really uncomfortable, that is sexual harassment, but then I don't know to what degree can this be, that they can get some kind of review. I've had instances where men touch me. They just touch me—they touch me all the time. It's usually in the way of being friendly, but then I feel like it should be some kind of gestures, like, they need to know that I'm okay with it before they do it. But I don't think that communication happens, necessarily.

Caroline shares with me a specific story that made her feel unsafe.

> One time I came into class and it was August, it was really hot. I was wearing shorts to class and I didn't really think of it as a problem to wear shorts. I'll wear whatever the fuck I want and I went into class wearing shorts because it was hot. One of my friends said, "Oh, I love your shorts. So cute." And then the instructor looked me up and down and said, "You call that a seminar outfit?" And I knew that he was joking, of course, but still I can't stop thinking about it, I can't forget that it happened—in public!... I didn't really call out the moment, which I feel bad for, but what can I do in that space? You have the positionality and power, am I going to call you out, you're a fucking sexist? I can't do that.

Caroline considers herself friends with this instructor and she feels that because of this friendship, he feels like he can get away with saying such things to her. "It's almost abusive because you get to feel this way because you're close to me and you feel like we can be friends, so you get to say whatever you want."

Jackie, a doctoral student about to defend her dissertation, tells me a story about the creative writing coordinator in her department feeling like he, too, is able to say whatever he wants without consequence. When they met in a bar for poetry readings, for instance,

> he asked me what kinds of films lesbians watched. I was just like, what do you mean, and he talked about *Blue is the Warmest Color* for a minute and talked about how artful that nine-minute sex scene was and is this the caliber of lesbian cinema? And I'm just thinking, that movie is terrible because it was directed by a man and we have heard stories about the abuse that went on behind the scenes, that this was just an elaborate male fantasy in film. He's talking about women scissoring my first semester here and I'm like, what?

And Jackie makes clear that it's not just men who harass women.

> There was a female grad student who basically kept harassing me, with some homophobia. It was incredibly awkward, looking up Instragram photos of my exes and commenting to me about their attractiveness and how they are in bed and things like that and what lesbian sex is like—and this is coming from a woman—and I was dissuaded from continuing with my effort to file a Title IX. By generally people within the department, not the Title IX office. They were interested in pursuing it, but the department was like, well, she's graduating.

In Jackie's case, the problem wasn't that people in her department didn't believe her, but rather that they saw that the "problem" was going to be going away, so why not just let it go? By this reasoning, any student could harass any other student in their final year of a program and face no repercussions because he or she is graduating and so somehow not a problem anymore. Until they get to the next place.

Eva, whose story I shared a little bit of earlier in this chapter, makes a point about the men in her department that I think applies to the men in many English departments:

> The men in this department believe that they can say whatever they want because they've reached a place beyond reprobation. So they are at the Ph.D. level, they are writing a creative dissertation, most of them have already written a book, even if it's not been published, they've written something that's that kind of length, so they think they've made it. So they can make rape jokes and they can make racist jokes and they can make homophobic jokes and they can make transphobic jokes and nobody says anything. Whereas when women make mistakes in this program, it's an immediate slap on the wrist.

I'm reminded here of Amanda's story from Chapter 3 wherein both she and a male graduate student colleague missed class because of a professional obligation and she was given extensive makeup work and he was given none. Men can say what they want, men can do what they want, and they will face no repercussions. Women, on the other hand, cannot. They must fulfill their roles as human givers.

Anna, an ABD doctoral student at a Research-2 university, tells me a story about what happened when she did not give in the ways she was expected to.

> When I withheld affection from someone in the program that I was in no way interested in, he spread a bunch of rumors about me and there was definitely personal fallout—he spread rumors about me wanting to sleep with him and he made a list of women that he thought wanted to sleep with him and he would tell everybody at parties. He's pretty sick, I think. But that was definitely a way of being shocked back into place because I then had the experience of all the new people in the cohort knew me by these rumors before they actually met me and of course everything blew over and everyone realized it wasn't true, but that sort of thing happened to a handful of women that I know.

Affection is one of the feminine-coded goods that women are expected to give to men, and when they withhold it, as in Anna's case, they are misogynistically punished. In Anna's case, she was punished by being characterized as sexually loose. As Lacy Crawford writes in her book *Notes on a Silencing*, "I believe, in fact, that the slur *slut* carries within it, Trojan-horse style, silence as its true intent. That the opposite of *slut* is not virtue but voice." To call Anna a slut, in not so many words, is to attempt to shut her up about her rejection of him. That it didn't work is a credit to Anna's refusal to submit to the norms of patriarchy.

Anna also has an uncomfortable relationship with a male faculty member who specializes in her primary area of study, nonfiction.

> We don't have a lot of professors and the professor that we do have has made me uncomfortable with the way he talks about my work as if I owe him something. I have a fellowship and he's said to me before that he was the reason I go the fellowship and he really wants to work with me. I know that's not true, but it still puts a lot of pressure on me. I also just don't always feel comfortable with him. I was in his office once. I was supposed to meet him and my friend was there and so on her way out I gave her a hug, and I guess my sweater came up on my side a little bit and when she left the room and closed the door, he asked, "Oh, what's that tattoo on your side?" I was like, oh my god, I'm wearing pants and a sweater, I just had to put my arms up really high to hug my friend, ahhh. I tried to—I never have my tattoos visible in the academic building for a reason, so calling attention to my body—it was just very uncomfortable and I know that's affected my work because he would be a person hopefully that I would be able to go to…but I don't feel comfortable…which is really sad.

The male professor sees no problem with remarking on a part of Anna's body that would normally remain covered, that she did not intentionally show him, and this understandably affects Anna's ability to work with him.

Also evident in the stories women told me about sexual harassment is just how long these incidents *stay* with them. Women who are now full professors told me stories from graduate school and their first few years on the tenure track. Here, for instance, is Erika, a full professor at a Research-2 university:

> Early in my grad school career, I was in my early 20s and I had written this paper for a film studies class and I really appreciated the opportunity—the course was on the film essay—I had no film studies background whatsoever—and the professor knew that I was interested in composition studies, so he allowed me to write this paper using composition concepts from the film essay to talk about this student writer I had been working with. It was the first time that I had ever gotten to write something that was kind of composition studies-ish as a grad student and he gave me this feedback that said, you know, this paper is really good, it has good potential, I really think that with some revision, it could be publishable. You should submit it to a journal.

Understandably, Erika was excited about this feedback, and she made an appointment to meet with her professor to get advice on revising her piece for publication.

> So I sit there and I've got my notebook on my lap and my pen and everything. And I'm 23, and this guy is, he's got three kids, this nice house, whatever, he's like probably my age now, and he says, "Is 11 am too early for a drink." But Amy, the saddest part of the story is that I went with him. I went and the next thing I know, I'm 23 years old, I'm sitting in this bar with this dude that I have absolutely zero interest in beyond what I was there for, which was, you said my paper could be publishable, how should I revise it. And we're sitting there in this bar, and he's talking and I can barely even hear what he's saying, it's going in one ear and out the other, he's talking about department politics and blah blah blah, stuff that I have no idea, and I'm just in my head, like, what are you doing? You don't want to sleep with this guy. What are you doing? Why are you here?

Erika struggles as she sits in the bar with her professor, not able to hear anything he is saying, wanting only to know whether her work is as good as he said it was.

> I just need to know whether the work is good. I don't need to know whether or not you want to fuck me. If you want a litmus test for whether or not sexism is real, the fact that you want to fuck me brings me down. It hurts me. It convinces me that, now I have to struggle with, maybe the paper wasn't really that good, maybe I'm not that smart, maybe it really isn't publishable. That becomes my burden to bear because you've taken this line.

Also worth noting is the frequency of the bar as a space where men do and say things they might not do or say otherwise. The bar is a space for flirting, for hook-ups, for drinking and losing inhibitions. The bar is not the academic office, full of books and papers. It is a space apart.

Erika recalls another incident, not long after she was a graduate student. She had been pregnant on her campus visit and then, months later when she started her job, "I received questions from two male colleagues, including the department chair, about whether or not I was nursing." Later in our conversation, she tells me, "One of the two senior male faculty who asked me about nursing would go on to be very flirty with me and then, on one occasion, a senior female faculty member said to me, of him, something like, watch out, he likes brunettes. It was gross."

Here's Dorothy, an emerita professor who had taught in her department for fifty years, recalling an incident from her graduate school days:

> When I was ready to do my dissertation and I wanted to write on C.S. Lewis and Tolkien science fiction and I was the only person at [institution] who had done anything with science fiction and I said I wanted to write on Lewis and Tolkien and the first thing he said was, "Oh, nobody's ever heard of them. You'll never make anything of yourself writing about that" because it was fantasy and maybe gendered too female. Then he looked at me and said, "Why does anyone who looks like you want to bother getting a doctorate?" He said it very winsomely. And I said, "Oh, Carl. Just be quiet. I'll pretend you didn't say that." Because that was the only way to cope with that. You sort of have to go along with it.

Rather than engaging with the content of what Dorothy wanted to work on, Carl points to her looks as a reason she shouldn't be getting a degree, evidencing his belief that women's job is to look good rather than to do the work of scholarship.

Both Miranda, a professor at a small liberal arts college, and Pam, a department chair whose story we heard part of earlier in this chapter, recall incidents from early in their first jobs out of graduate school. Miranda tells me,

> My first job. There was the poetry reading where I sit down and the drunken poet comes in and sits down—he's also been behaving in a really curious way to me that I wasn't, I was too naïve to understand what was happening—but at any rate, one piece of this story is that he comes in to the poetry reading, he sits down, and he basically just drapes himself all over my body in public. One of my dear male colleagues basically gets up…and simply makes him move over and sits down beside me.

Miranda's inability to take up physical space but for the intrusion of a man is echoed in Pam's story.

> In my previous department, there was a distinguished professor who was a poet and he was diagnosed with MS eventually and I think he had some dementia but he had a long history of harassment before that. What he would do was he would park his chair right in my door and he would start reciting poetry and I had to guess who the poets were. And he got to the point where he was doing the same poets over again and he'd be like, wow, you have a remarkable memory. I complained about his behavior and I was the one who had to move my office to another building while he was left where he was.

When I express my horror at Pam's situation, she responds, "I would just say, could you please move. I have to go to the bathroom. Because I just felt—I mean, I was trapped. I guess I could have leaped over him somehow, but." In her book,

On Violence and On Violence Against Women, Jacqueline Rose writes about sexual harassment that it "is always a sexual demand, but it also carries a more sinister and pathetic injunction: 'You will think about me.' Like sexual abuse, to which it is affiliated, harassment brings mental life to a standstill, destroying the mind's capacity for reverie" (37). In Pam's case—as in so many of these cases—the senior professor colonizes the young professor's physical and mental space by not allowing her to leave her own office. Never mind reverie.

And finally, Meg tells me about a member of her department who also had no compunction about getting up in women's space:

> At conferences we literally had to devise this system of hand signals to the other men around. Because he'd come around and he'd be really physically aggressive with you even in very public places and he'd be pretty drunk and so then had to like broadcasts to the nearest safe guy. So we had designated men who would then come and take him away from you. That went on for years.

So many women I spoke with remembered these incidents from graduate school or from early in their careers at their first jobs. The contemporaneous stories I heard from senior women faculty were more likely to be about witnessing colleagues' harassment of others, as I detailed earlier in this chapter. But what all of these stories have in common is that they indicate men's feelings of entitlement to women's bodies, to their affection and attention, and to their space. They show us that, even in spaces like English departments, where we might expect things to be just a fraction better than spaces outside the academy, women are seen, first and foremost, as bodies to which men are entitled. In Rose's words, they show us that these spaces of progressive politics are not free from sexual harassment as "the great male performative, the act through which a man aims to convince his target not only that he is the one with power, which is true, but also that his power and his sexuality are one and the same thing" (38).

References

Crawford, Lacy. *Notes on a Silencing*. New York: Little, Brown and Company, 2020.
Deer, Sarah, and Bonnie Clairmont. "*Gossip* Is an English Word." *Believe Me*. Ed. Jessica Valenti and Jaclyn Friedman. New York: Seal Press, 2020. 15–24.
Ericsson, Patricia Freitag, Ed. *Sexual Harassment and Cultural Change in Writing Studies*. Fort Collins, CO: The WAC Clearinghouse, 2020.

Friedman, Jaclyn. "The Cost of Disbelieving." *Believe Me*. Ed. Jessica Valenti and Jaclyn Friedman. New York: Seal Press, 2020. 299–307.

Gilmore, Leigh. *Tainted Witness: Why We Doubt What Women Say About Their Lives*. New York: Columbia UP, 2017.

Manne, Kate. *Entitled: How Male Privilege Hurts Women*. New York: Crown, 2020.

Micciche, Laura. "From the Editor." *Composition Studies* 46.2 (2018): 10–11.

Rose, Jacqueline. *On Violence and On Violence Against Women*. New York: Farrar, Straus, and Giroux, 2021.

5

On Gaslighting

> In the years since I've been noticing these kinds of things, I've sort of moved from thinking it's my problem or there's something wrong with me to actually saying, no, this is not wrong with me, this is wrong with the place I work.
>
> —Rebecca, associate professor

> The first rule of misogyny is that you do not complain about such mistreatment.
>
> —Kate Manne, *Entitled*

I shared in Chapter 1 part of Susan's story of department meetings in which "there's a lot of sexual content that's really inappropriate. Making comments like, 'Oh, such-and-such student was wearing a really low tank top and that was just'—very much objectifying women and their bodies in a department meeting." Later in her interview, Susan shared with me that she protested this kind of talk in a couple department meetings by walking out.

> I slammed whatever I had in my hands down on the table and said, "This is the most inappropriate thing. I can't believe it. I don't consider any of you colleagues. You're all sexist, chauvinist pigs." I got written up for being unprofessional. I had several marks against me. I got written up for being—I had to meet with the president—for not showing collegial behavior, not being professional, and there are other things. But again, if you're going to yell at people and tell them they're being chauvinist pigs, you have to be a man in order to do that. If a woman does that, they're stepping out of line.

Susan is one among many of the women I spoke with who protested misogynistic behavior and were punished for it. As Kate Manne writes and I have noted earlier in this book, "misogyny is a self-masking phenomenon: trying to draw attention to the phenomenon is liable to give rise to more of it" (xix).

Rebecca, an associate professor at a liberal arts college, tells me that when she points to misogyny in her department,

> people will say, oh, you're attacking your colleagues, you're basically destroying all the work they've done recently, but I'm just like, but the work they've done is

not in the interest of anyone. It's not like people are like, oh, you should just calm down. They do say that. But it's also this attack mode that comes as a result. The dissuasion is more explicit by saying you're not playing by the team rules. I think that's much worse than saying, oh, you should just be quiet.

When Rebecca points to the ways her colleagues are acting misogynistically, she is told that no, it is actually Rebecca herself who is doing the attacking. She is the one doing wrong. Jill, an associate professor at a Research-1 university, tells me that when she protested misogynistic behavior to her feminist chair, she (the chair) told Jill to be nicer to her male colleague. She "told me to be the caretaker."

For some of the women I spoke with, the very idea of reporting the misogyny they'd experienced in their departments was squashed at the outset. "I have been cautioned against making waves," Patricia tells me. "I was told my first year by my dean that we're not used to junior faculty members calling attention to themselves….I'm supposed to offer respect to people." Patricia is the same person I wrote about in Chapter 3 whose department has a civility contract that functions as a kind of threat for women. "Any time that we step out of line we are threatened with being uncivil." Two graduate students used the language of "rocking the boat." Amanda told me, "I have been encouraged to keep quiet by my peers as well. Don't rock the boat and of course, I also feel like my position itself discourages me from rocking any boats because I'm in a fairly identifiable position because I'm the only person in my specialization at my level anymore. Anything I say that comes with any commentary about what my specialization is, identifies me." Eva, too, used this language. She told me that she heard over and over,

> Don't rock the boat, don't put anybody at risk, don't say the things that need to be said because they haven't been said yet and we just need to get through this fucking program. Buckle down and deal. It's the exact same shit I saw in undergrad when I came forward then. This is what I have seen when it comes to misogyny and I have been speaking out about it my whole life and facing the same reaction.

In her work on complaint, Sara Ahmed reflects on the implications of the language of *rocking the boat*:

> A complaint is heard as making waves: as stopping things from being steady. Keeping things steady here is the requirement to make things light; to laugh it off; to grin and bear it. A complaint is implied to be what sticks—it might not be on your CV; but you will always be known for it. *A complaint is sticky data.* You will become not only a complainer but a complaint in the sense of a minor but

irritating ailment or condition. The implication here is that rocking as a motion is more dangerous for those with less stable footing. Warnings are thus used *to heighten your consciousness of the precarity of your situation*. They are also being used to put people in place; to tell you who is bigger and who is smaller (they are bigger; you are smaller) or who will prevail and who will not (they will prevail; you will not). In other words, warnings can be how some are put in their place by being told how easy it would be for them to lose their footing. ("Warnings")

The message behind "don't rock the boat" is to keep things running smoothly, to maintain the status quo, to just get through the day, the week, the semester.

Being silenced in this way, being told over and over again that what is happening to you is not actually happening to you, that it is not worth identifying, responding to, or reporting, is a form of gaslighting that leads to women's questioning their own ability to understand themselves. In this chapter, I share stories about women's experiences with gaslighting in English departments. First I share stories about what happens when women are individually told that what is happening to them is not, in fact, happening to them. I explore how this affects their understanding of themselves as actors in the world. I then analyze two forms of leverage used to gaslight further. The first form of leverage stems from the deeply held belief that women cannot be misogynists, so when women experience misogyny from other women, they second-guess their experiences. And the second form of leverage stems from the pervasive belief that English departments are committed to social justice, diversity, and inclusivity. When women experience misogyny in departments whose commitments to these values are explicit, they lend more credence to the departments' vision and second-guess their own experiences.

Women Questioning Themselves

The colloquial understanding of gaslighting works in the situations I share here. A woman experiences something in the workplace. When she shares her experience with others, she is told that, actually, what she believes happened to her didn't happen. It was not misogyny, it was *something else*. Someone else describes the woman's experience in a way that causes her to question her understanding of reality. Crucially, this alternate description of the woman's experience ascribes all nefarious intent to the victim, the woman sharing her story in the first place. Kate Abramson, in her landmark essay, "Turning Up the Lights on Gaslighting," writes that one of the things gaslighting refuses its target is interpersonal confirmation of one's sense of reality: gaslighting happens "when the interpersonal confirmation is refused, or deliberately thwarted, precisely in order to radically undermine someone's standing to protest bad conduct" (6). One of my interviewees, Lucy, makes very clear that what she needed when she experienced misogyny in her workplace was just this kind of interpersonal confirmation: "I have to talk about what is happening, which is just reliving it for me, but it's important because I need these people to say, yes, that was wrong, if it comes to it, I'll say it's wrong."

Abramson also explains that gaslighting leads to accusations that a woman is "being crazy, oversensitive, paranoid." What these characterizations have in common, she explains, "is that they are ways of charging someone not simply with being *wrong* or *mistaken*, but being in no condition to judge whether she is wrong or mistaken." The target of gaslighting cannot even know herself.

> The accusations are about the target's basic rational competence—her ability to get facts right, to deliberate, her basic evaluative competencies and ability to react appropriately: her independent standing as deliberator and moral agent. When gaslighting succeeds, it drives its targets crazy in the sense of deeply undermining just these aspects of a person's independent standing. (8)

> *You're being oversensitive.*
> *I think you misunderstood.*
> *He didn't really mean it.*

Abramson notes that gaslighting can function to "reinforce the very sexist norms which the target was trying to resist and/or those on which the gaslighter relies in his/her manipulations of the target" (3), and in the contexts with which we are concerned here, gaslighting is particularly egregious for its calling into question a woman's basic competence.

Moira, an associate professor at a Research-1 university, tells me about an instance of gaslighting at her previous institution, where a senior male faculty member asked her to make photocopies.

> I went and told the chair and she was like, "You must have misunderstood." She was an out lesbian, feminist, worked on Audre Lorde, and I just couldn't believe her answer. The associate chair was similar. She was like, "Oh, he was probably confused. He probably thought you were the department secretary"—as if that was some sort of excuse.

Moira's competence as a rational deliberator is called into question by both her chair and her associate chair. Stephanie, also an associate professor at a Research-1 university, tells me that among her female colleagues, she talks about what's happening and they call it what it is.

> My female colleagues and I talk about it a lot. We call it what it is, whether it's misogyny or ableism or racism....Whenever any of us complained about Neal, Diane [her department chair] would be like, Now that's not really…I've been gaslit a lot. Now that's not really what's happening here. You're just being difficult, kind of thing.

You're being oversensitive. You're being difficult. You. You. You. It's all on you.

Beth, a fourth-year doctoral student at a Research-2 university, shares a classic story of gaslighting.

> I asked that a male faculty person not be allowed to edit my work on a public facing document without first speaking to me about the changes he wished to make. I asked this because I spent a considerable amount of time on the document and had received marketing training from the university on how to write the document that the male faculty person refused to undergo. I was told by my male supervisor that if I was going to get upset about it, that I should go speak to the faculty person in question myself. I was not upset. I was making a professional request, but my emotions were brought into the situation and I was made to feel as if I was overreacting.

In Beth's case, reacting at all is equated to overreacting. Reacting at all is characterized as being "upset," and being upset is understood to be irrational. Beth tells me that this situation "made me question my thinking and it also told me that my supervisor did not value my knowledge or ability, since he didn't trust me or seem to want to listen to me." This is one of the effects of gaslighting: it causes women to question themselves, to doubt themselves, to wonder at their own competence. I saw this a number of times during my interviews. Even women who did not speak explicitly about gaslighting told me about the ways they had begun to doubt their own abilities and competence, their sense of self, as a result of the misogyny they'd experienced.

Jody, a community college department chair, found herself saying, "There must be something wrong with me personally. Like, why am I bad at this job? Why am I not qualified for this job, even though—I am." And Alyssa, an associate professor at a Research-2 university, tells me, "I'm just so sick of always trying to prove myself. I'm not doing it anymore because I've done it so many times through emails and I've had to say, Hey, what I'm doing is also important, but it's also infantilizing a little bit." After the experience I shared in Chapter 1, Molly tells me,

> It definitely made me start questioning my own personality even. It made me question, maybe I am cold. Maybe I do have resting bitch face. Maybe people are intimidated by me. It made me question that professionally.... But it really—I didn't want to let it hurt me, but it did. I don't want to be thought of as some coldhearted bitch. It made me, I think, for the first week or two afterward, examine every interaction I had with everyone. Was I friendly enough to that person? Did I smile at them? Did I use a tone of voice that could be construed as angry, uninterested, or whatever? ... Questioning those kinds of things that I know aren't true and that I know are in place for my own mental wellbeing, but it really made me—maybe I do need to act a little more feminine around here. Maybe I'll be perceived better by coworkers, by my own students, by everyone. Luckily, my partner was like, No. You don't have to change who you are because of one old man's opinion.

All three of these women doubt themselves, doubt their abilities, and question their interpretation of reality. And Eva, a first-year doctoral student, found herself questioning herself *while talking to me*:

> Even now, speaking to somebody that I know completely understands where I'm coming from, I find myself changing the situation from, I got fucked over in a program that wasn't ready to take care of me to, this is my fault because this is a situation I created.

Eva is clearly demonstrating signs here of having internalized sexist norms that would have her taking the blame for any situation about which she may have reason to complain.

Women Engaging in Misogyny

Recall that Manne conceptualizes misogyny as the law enforcement branch of patriarchy, responsible for enforcing gender norms having to do, primarily, with women's obligations and men's entitlement. Women are obligated to *give* feminine-coded goods and services, and men are entitled to *take* masculine-coded goods and services. When these norms are challenged, misogyny comes along to shock a woman back into place. There is nothing, then, that precludes women from engaging in misogyny. Women who play by the rules of patriarchy will be rewarded and may act to shock other women back into place. Abramson writes about the tools gaslighters use to manipulate their targets—among them love, empathy, and authority—and to that list I want to add the pervasive belief that women do not engage in misogyny. Abramson characterizes these tools as leverage, and says that, for instance, loving someone "plausibly gives us reason to give their views a little extra credence." Love is a reason a woman might second-guess herself when she finds herself questioning something he says. Because so many of us (want to) believe that women have one another's backs, we find it harder to believe that a woman might engage in misogynistic behavior toward us. We thus second-guess our own understanding of reality more than we would when a man acts in the same way. Almost a third of the women I spoke with mentioned women's misogynistic behavior toward other women; many of these women expressed some kind of surprise when doing so, which I took to be evidence of the belief that women do not engage in misogyny.

Here's Jody: "To be honest, a lot of the misogyny that I've experienced comes from my female colleagues, not my male colleagues." Jackie, an ABD doctoral student, says, "It's so weird because it has come from women in the department as well as men. They should be on our side, but they absolutely are not." She continues, "I get comments from female faculty like, why did you cut off all your hair? You looked so pretty.... Several times I've had to deal with female and male faculty commenting on my appearance and the fact that it is not feminine at times and I'm just like, there are other dykes in the department, wtf?" Rebecca also uses the term "weird" to describe women engaging in misogyny:

> I think the thing that is always most fascinating to me is that the kind of misogyny that I'm experiencing in my department is partially coming from other women versus the men, which I think is really, really interesting. We're two men and four women, and I'm clearly the least female presenting female in the department and I'm also the one who's always at the center of all sorts of controversies and things like that partially due to the fact that I don't fall into adoration and things like that. So the other women are attacking me for not falling along the gender roles. It's a very weird situation.

Alyssa asked me, as we spoke, "When you talk about misogyny, do you include women?" and then told me about a female faculty member back in graduate school.

> She had all these ideas about why my advisor was really supporting me. He was supporting everyone, really, but she was very jealous and very hostile towards me. Cornered me at this big conference, tried to ask me a bunch of questions about my relationship with him and then she posted some hate comments, actually. She made it very clear that she was anti-Semitic and my session in this very big conference mysteriously got canceled and someone posted a big poster saying that this session was canceled and I immediately thought it must be her. So I talked to the organizers and I undid that, but it was really distressing. I was really stressed out by the way she was treating me.

There's an obvious power imbalance between a female faculty member and a female graduate student, and we can see that power imbalance playing itself out misogynistically in Alyssa's case.

Even as female graduate students are learning about power and about feminism and the patriarchy, they see the ways the women around them are leveraging the belief that women support women to their advantage. Here's Laura, a third-year doctoral student at a Research-2 university: "There are females in leadership roles, especially women who would probably characterize themselves as second-wave feminists, that will take on the mantle of the patriarchy and discriminate against women—other women in the department. Junior faculty, graduate students." And Jeanne, a second-year doctoral student, agrees: "In terms of leadership, a lot of women, as you would see in any business or non-academic setting, have worked their way to the top by taking on what we would code as masculine qualities, and they make themselves untouchable by calling themselves feminist." Anna, an ABD doctoral student, tells me about the pressure she felt from other women about her situation:

> People were pressuring me to go to Title IX and they were all women who were claiming to be very supportive to women and progressive with their practices and the theory they were reading, but the problem was that they were trying to bully me into doing something that should have been entirely my own decision.

The *theory they were reading* doesn't often translate to practices, it seems. Laura puts it this way: "If you are studying language, especially if you are studying anything that qualifies as feminist, um, that doesn't mean you carry that into your life. So I think it hurts more because you expect that they would." We expect that the work feminists do would carry into their lives, that women would treat other women with respect and dignity, but they don't always do this, even in the academic workplace.

I shared parts of Lucy's story in Chapter 3; Lucy told me that she often feels like she is in an abusive relationship at work because her WPA punishes her whenever she is assertive or stands up for herself. Of her WPA, Lucy says, "For me, it's always a little bit worse when the misogynist at work is the woman and not the man. One who's always railing against the ways she's been treated because she's a woman. She has no concept of what's happening. I don't even think she gets it. She's so deep in the system." Michelle echoes Lucy's characterization of women-on-women misogyny as the worst: "The worst is that it was female—so it's not just guys that do it. There's this expectation that women are always going to support women, that that's what they're supposed to do even if you don't agree with them, even if they're wrong, you're still supposed to support them because they're women." Of this expectation, Stephanie says,

> Part of the thing about this discipline [rhetoric and composition] is that it is largely founded by and run by women, with the expectation that there's an implicit belief that women can't be misogynists. The worst structural misogyny in this department is perpetrated by women.

It hurts more when the pushback comes from other women precisely because we carry with us the belief that women can't be misogynists. So we tend to give more credence to the things women say to us, we tend to have more reason to believe them, and thus we are more easily gaslighted, questioning our understanding of our own reality. When what we see and what we believe to be true do not match, which are we to believe? When we have been living in a patriarchy our whole lives, where "it's part of the structure of sexism that women are supposed to be less confident, to doubt our views, beliefs, reactions, and perceptions, more than men" (Abramson 22), it is easier to gaslight us with the pervasive belief that women cannot be misogynists.

English Departments as Spaces of Diversity, Equity, and Inclusion

The second form of leverage used to gaslight women who experience misogyny in English departments is a department's stated commitment to diversity, equity, inclusion, and social justice. Of the thirty-nine women I interviewed, thirty-five told me that their departments publicly claimed to value social justice, inclusivity, and equity, and many, without my prompting, went on to tell me that these commitments were often in name only. In Alyssa's words, "I think these values are not really enacted or…it doesn't really make me feel better in my everyday life." Some interviewees distinguished between sentiment and practice, as Erika does here: "We're still sort of developing this language, but I think that it is a shared sentiment. Whether or not it's a shared practice, I can't entirely say." Of her department, Anna says, "I don't know how it's always executed in the department, but there is an awareness of those things being important." Eva says, "We have faculty members whose work does that, but it's something that I think our program wants to think that it is, but it's definitely not. Not at all."

But the stated commitment at some schools is strong. Stephanie tells me, "I think some faculty consider [these values] to be the centerpiece of the program. It's something that's very much understood and publicly espoused to be very much a part of our culture, our curriculum, and the ethos of the department." Though I asked the question about the extent to which interviewees' departments value social justice, inclusivity, and diversity, many women told me that that commitment shows up most often in curriculum. Lucy tells me, "In the revised curriculum for the whole of the department of English, it's a goal to teach inclusivity and diversity, to add in more people of color and things into all of the courses we teach, not just, so the literature courses need to include more diversity, when we choose texts for our comp classes, we need to make sure we pay attention to those things." Alexandra says of her department, "One of the first ways we've talked about cultural inclusivity is we just redid our first-year composition assessment outcomes and one of the new outcomes is addressing multiculturalism and cultural competencies. We did that in part—gender, race, class, all of those things—we did that in part because it's a university wide goal." Miranda tells me, "Equality—that's also in our goals, especially in our curriculum. We want a curriculum that's attendant to issues of diversity and social justice, it's sort of built into the language that is there." Angela tells me, "We speak a lot about the diverse literature that we teach in our courses."

It is this stated commitment that appears so frequently and that provides so much of the ethos of English departments that functions as leverage in some of the gaslighting that women experience in their workplaces. When they are surrounded by the discourse of diversity, equity, and inclusion at the same time that they are experiencing misogyny, they may second-guess themselves about what is real. As Rebecca puts it,

> I don't think we're aware of the kinds of ways in which we're not really endorsing equality on different levels. We pay lip service to it…. An English department

devoted to social justice should be a place in which social justice is like, part of what's going on in the department, but often times it is not. It's like maybe we do stuff for the outside world, but on the inside, we are basically like a medieval society.

Rebecca's point about doing stuff for the outside world is worth highlighting here; we may be committed to social justice and diversity for *our students*, but when it comes to one another, to our colleagues, we do not often see this commitment spelled out. Gwen makes the important point that for some departments, when it comes to employees behaving misogynistically toward one another,

> we have difficulty naming things and people who are bullying or not kind and not considerate of others are able to do that because they're not called on the carpet because it feels like the standard we use is a standard of what's legal. Bullying can be legal. It has to be so severe for it to get to the point of not being legal. It just feels like a whole bunch of stuff gets to happen because it's not illegal.

If it's not illegal, it is usually allowed to continue to happen, with women being gaslighted into believing that what is happening is not actually happening. Marie puts it this way:

> I think there's this masking that happens in a department such as English where diversity is valued or spoken of as highly valuable to ignore it—it's not just ignoring, it's like an active pretending that it's not happening. It's an active sweeping under the rug. It feels like a gaslighting thing. No, no, no, you don't understand. That's not happening.

It's the commitment itself—the discourse of diversity and social justice— that leads to sweeping misogyny under the rug. We cannot admit that this is happening.

English departments are not the only departments with a stated commitment to diversity and social justice, of course. But there's something about the combination of English departments' stated commitment and their refusal to acknowledge the problem that leads to even more harm. A few women explicitly told me that people, especially men, in English departments do not believe they are misogynistic, and so would not believe they have anything to remedy. Moira says, "I think the biggest problem in academe in terms of misogyny is that the men all think they're not misogynistic." Miranda tells me, "Others would deny that it's misogyny. I feel like you're allowed to say that things are racist, but misogynist, no. People will be really quick to deny that." Lillian had an extended response to this issue:

> The objects of analysis are out there and we talk the talk but then we don't walk the walk. I love being a scholar and a teacher, don't get me wrong, but I have a little bit of a love/hate relationship with the university because I think that we have such an arrogance that we feel…it's part of our training, it's part of the culture of the western university, we have such arrogance in thinking that we're not part of the problem, too. That we have all the answers. I won't go down the road that conservative critics of the academy go down where they're all, they're a bunch of liberals who aren't in touch with the real world, but we're kind of in some ways sometimes not in touch with the real world…. And it's easy to analyze and then critique that which we see as distanced from ourselves. Then we turn the mirror on ourselves and things get really, really uncomfortable really fast.

I like Lillian's language of turning the mirror on ourselves. We are not, as she says, very good at doing that. Monica echoes this point when she says, "I think the problem with English departments is that we often do see ourselves as more inclusive and more liberal and so if there's misogyny, they're like, it wouldn't be in our department, we're asking people to read *The New Jim Crow* and consider all of these things."

Rebecca makes a couple of important points when she says,

> You're fighting for inclusion in a work setting while you're also fighting for inclusion of the group of people you're part of in the stuff you're teaching. I think that's what makes English departments in particular prone to these types of moves. I do think that you could say it's the same in other nooks of academia, too, but I think in the sciences, people are not surprised at the misogyny. When someone says, oh, you know, I'm a Ph.D. biologist and people in my life make fun of me, people are just like, oh yeah, scientists, but if you say, I work in an English department and people seem to make fun of me for gender all the time, and people are like, but it's an English department, isn't that where all the liberals walk around? You're inhabiting a space that's already considered to be progressive. I think as a discipline English is not progressive at all.

While many of my interviewees told me that they think misogyny is not particular to English departments, that it is surely a problem in the STEM fields, Rebecca's point that we are maybe not *surprised* by the misogyny in the STEM fields is an important one. We expect English departments to be progressive. Here's Lisa: "I would like to say that I would think that I would be less of an issue in English departments, where we study people with diverse experiences and we read books about…but I don't necessarily think that's true."

Stephanie, though, was not surprised. She says, "I don't know if it's because I came up through scientific and technical programs that I *did* expect it, but what I find more annoying and more violent is that we can't admit it because we perceive ourselves this way. We can't say here are all the instances and here are the problems with hiring, and they'll say, well, that's not what that means." The denial is made a little bit easier in English departments, too, because the misogyny is often, according to some of the women I spoke with, more covert than overt. Here's Elizabeth: "I would say it's a problem more generally, it just seems more covert in English departments because a lot of people think of English departments as being more liberal and more liberal minded and so it becomes a little more insidious because it's not so blatant." Three women pointed to English department members' facility with language as a reason the misogyny can be so insidious. Here's Jill: "Because English people are so good with language, they can be particularly cutting and sideways in the way they go about it because they know they can't do it directly." Here's Gwen:

> A lot of time people in English departments have a facility with language—the verbal gymnastics and the semantics, the many, many ways of diminishing one's colleagues without just outright doing it. People seem to be smart enough that there's a line, so they do what they need to do not to cross it legally. People are a bit more slippery in their dealings, so they're harder to pin down. In some other departments, where they're not as attuned to these things, they will be much more bald, obvious.

And Alexandra makes a very specific case for the ways we in English departments could be using our skills to work toward more equity.

> What's more frustrating to me about English departments is because we study language—we study how language shapes discourse and personhood—it seems like the English department should be the place where we really interrogate how we speak to one another and how we encode these issues in annual reviews and policies and stuff like that. When I see an English department not engaging in those critical conversations, it's like, what are we doing? You're the first faculty member to tear apart a poem for its misogyny, but when it comes to doing an annual review, you're like, well, your male students say you did a feminist review…and you're like, *what*? So a text is a text is a text. Let's apply these kinds of ideas to the texts of higher education.

And that really is the crux of it: we say one thing and do another. We ask students to engage in critical thinking about issues of diversity and equity, but when we find ourselves faced with misogyny in our departments, the first move we often make is to deny. We fall back on our stated commitments to social justice and diversity, and we believe that that rhetorical move will somehow work its way into our interpersonal dealings with one another.

Of all the women I spoke with, Amanda, a third-year doctoral student, put the issue most succinctly when she said,

> There's a special kind of gaslighting that's enabled when an academic can claim a scholar persona that's dedicated to X social justice cause, and that persona is used to invalidate experiential perceptions of that person as a departmental figure/colleague/mentor/professor. So, a scholar who claims commitment to feminism may cry and ask a female grad student to help her understand why her students don't experience her as transformative—expecting emotional labor from that grad student—but that student's interpretation of the incident is gaslighted by their knowledge of the scholar persona, which suggests that this professor surely wasn't expecting emotional labor from a female body, that it must be something else, that the student is simply *wrong* about what's happening. Sometimes this happens silently, and sometimes it's vocalized (the scholar persona is explicitly invoked as a defense), but when it happens systemically in a department heavily populated with people who can claim social justice scholarship, it creates an environment that is especially toxic and ripe for both enabling misogyny and silencing its victims.

A faculty member who dedicates her work to social justice causes would, we can presume, be committed in her everyday life to social justice. This belief, however, is dependent on the assumption that we live what we study, that we enact what we study. Kate Manne writes, in *Entitled*, of a woman who told her story to *Vox* magazine. She had finally shared, in couples counseling, her "deepest darkest truth": "she had felt sexually violated by her husband all throughout their eight-year marriage." Manne narrates the story:

> And yet, for the fifteen years following that counseling session, these awful realities were almost impossible for her to acknowledge. She was afraid to tell her husband that she didn't want to have sex with him; she was afraid to reject him; and she was even afraid to admit to herself what was happening. Instead, she writes, "I bargained my way out of sex as often as I could. I gloried in being sick enough to have the right to refuse," even though "I knew, intellectually, I was entitled to refuse sex" at any time.

There were times when she couldn't refuse, however, and she let him have sex with her, "while she read a book to distract herself." The story continues in this way, and it is only the advent of the MeToo movement that prompts the woman to reconsider what she is doing. Manne writes, "This story goes to show just how difficult it can be for a woman to resist a sense of male sexual entitlement that she has internalized, on his behalf." But then, in the next paragraph, Manne writes,

> The kicker? The author, who remained anonymous, is a humanities professor who regularly teaches feminist theory. But, she confesses, "All the feminist texts I read could not drown out what I had absorbed from society and popular culture: that it was my duty to satisfy my husband, regardless of my own feelings." (67–8)

Perhaps we, too—members of English departments—have absorbed messages from society and popular culture that our feminist texts and our commitments to social justice cannot drown out. Perhaps the real achievement in this woman's story is that she *recognized* the disconnect between what she teaches and how she acts; this is what I hope this work will help us do.

When women feel gaslighted by their own departments' stated commitments to diversity, inclusivity and social justice, they do not feel safe sharing what is happening to them. About her department, Alyssa says,

> It's not a safe space, it's very threatening. You don't want to share your stories. You don't feel like if you share your story, people will care or respect or maybe it will actually backfire if you tell those stories. That's why I call these spaces unsafe spaces for me. So you can create your own little pockets of spaces. But it's still stressful in that way.

Echoing Alyssa's concerns, Kristie, a non-tenure-track professor who was laid off from her public university, tells me, when I ask if she had shared her story with anybody else,

> There's one person in the department that I've told I'm answering these questions today—a full professor who I would trust with my life, kind of person. Other than that, no. I'm afraid of these people. I feel like I'm starring in The Godfather. And maybe I've become paranoid and I'm constantly trying to evaluate my paranoia level, but it seems so—the system just seems so corrupt. And I have to say, I have a therapist that I've had for several years who will tell me that it's like a dysfunctional family. She used the word *corrupt* herself. I feel better that a professional sees it that way—in the sense that I'm not crazy.

Kristie needs her understanding of reality confirmed by another person, someone who is outside of her department; it is this interpersonal confirmation that is so often denied to women who are gaslighted, as Abramson points out, and it is this interpersonal confirmation that assures women that they are not crazy.

Anticipating Gaslighting for This Work

As I work on this book and on this chapter specifically, I cannot help but anticipate the ways I will be gaslighted for exposing the misogynistic underbelly of English departments. I can imagine the responses:

You're being oversensitive.
You're overanalyzing.
You're going to make trouble for English departments.
That's not how it is here.
I've had to deal with much worse.
Things used to be so much worse.
Why are you attacking us?
Why are you so angry?

And there have been times when I've been writing when I've found myself gaslighting myself.

Does any of this really matter in the scheme of things?

Abramson writes about the sexist norm of self-doubt, and I am not immune from it; I, too, doubt my views and my perceptions even as I share the stories of women who have trusted me with their stories. What if I'm interpreting these stories wrong? What if they're not actually misogyny and they can be explained in some other way? What if, what if, what if.

I work in a department that has subtly been knocking me down over the years, from a colleague telling me that the department needed more people like me who just put their heads down and did their jobs, to another colleague revealing that she would never pass the exams of any of the graduate students I worked with, to my supervisor calling me inappropriate for asking about my annual evaluation letter. These and other comments like them add up to the point where I begin to question my abilities as a teacher and scholar. I begin to wonder if I'm up to the task of caring for these stories. The very reasons I wanted to do this work—that I was tired of both experiencing and witnessing the misogyny in my own department—made me question whether I should or could even do it. And so misogyny writes its way into this very book.

The year 2020 was a hard one for this project; living through the pandemic, I suddenly felt like paying attention to misogyny in English departments was a luxury nobody needed me to attend to. I felt like I was indulging myself by paying attention to stories that had nothing to do with people getting sick and dying. But the stories I was attending to have everything to do with people getting sick and dying. We just don't talk about it.

References

Abramson, Kate. "Turning Up the Lights on Gaslighting." *Philosophical Perspectives* 28 (2014): 1–30.
Ahmed, Sara. "Warnings." *Feminist Killjoys*, 3 Dec. 2018.
Manne, Kate. *Entitled: How Male Privilege Hurts Women*. New York: Crown, 2020.

6

Women No Longer Want to Give

Women were promised we could "have it all." We've discovered that means "doing it all" instead. And not only do we now get to do it all, but we do so for lower pay and less recognition, and not at all surprisingly, at the expense of our health.

—Lisa Mosconi, Ph.D., *The XX Brain*

If we're not going to get sympathetic witnessing, it's okay, forget it, I just won't. But then what it means is, we cannot be fully present. We cannot be there. So they lose out on everything that we have to offer.

—Gwen, associate professor

Rebecca tells me about the constellation of effects she attributes to her experiences with misogyny.

It took me a long time to actually realize this was going on. I think it took me about five to six years of working here until I understood how gender played such an important role, and the reason I started seeing it is I'm actually active in the union, and the union is even more misogynistic than my department, so I was basically encountering similar situations where before I could say, "Oh, it's just the people I work with," versus going to a different setting, and it was different people with all the same attitudes, sort of replicating this same kind of world. That's how I started thinking about it. I think at first I was shocked. And so work became very difficult and tedious and at the same time I developed depression and anxiety... there was just a total overload. That's kind of what it felt like. It also affected my personal life—I was completely not interested in doing anything anymore because my work life was so bad. What that of course means is that my scholarship is down. I'm slowly getting back into writing, but there's a long gap where nothing actually happened. I tried to fit in and figure out how to deal with the situation I'm in and make it work, but it didn't really because there's no recognition that the situation exists—misogyny versus my personal issue or something like that. That made it so hard to work through.

We can see a kind of circular effect in Rebecca's experience: work was bad, which affected her personal life, which affected her scholarship. Rebecca notes that it took her a long time to realize what was going on, and it is my hope that her story, and others like hers, can help readers identify what is happening around them much more readily. Further, what made Rebecca's situation worse was that nobody around her recognized that misogyny was at play.

It should come as no surprise to any reader who has made it this far that misogyny is exhausting and time-consuming, and that one of the biggest effects of it on women's lives is a decreased desire to continue giving of themselves at work. One of my biggest takeaways from this work is that *we are missing out*—we are missing out on the creativity, ingenuity, inspiration, dedication, and enthusiasm that so many women come to their graduate programs and careers with. These beautiful characteristics are beaten out of us when the system we thought was structured by progressive values turns out, instead, to be shaped by the belief that women should be human givers rather than human beings. Some of us come to English departments perhaps a bit naïve, wanting to believe, as Brianna wanted to believe, "although I knew it wasn't true—that I wouldn't end up in a department where such overt sexism would be happening," where there's this expectation "that you'll maintain this façade that everything is fine, that no one's racist, that no one's sexist, or any of those things."

We are missing out because we are working in departments rife with misogyny whose effects on women are substantial; women's health is suffering, they want to engage less in the work of their departments, and they are unable to conduct research in ways they used to be able to. Further, they are putting off making important life decisions for fear of the repercussions such decisions may have on their careers. And most significantly, women are leaving their jobs and academia altogether.

Effects on Women's Health

Thirteen of the thirty-nine women—fully one-third—I spoke with indicated that the misogyny they'd experienced at work led to physical and mental health problems. We have heard stories about the rise, among student populations, of anxiety and related mental health problems, and this anxiety was something that, as teachers themselves, a number of my interviewees raised. They are concerned about students' anxiety. But they are also suffering from anxiety themselves. Lucy, for instance, tells me, "I have just had to up my antidepressants and restart my anxiety medicine because every time I get an email from my WPA, I get really, like, panicky." Lucy's anxiety also leads to exhaustion: "I've been really tired at the end of the day because I feel like I've had to wear armor at work. It just feels really heavy." Similarly, Susan tells me

> This job has absolutely stressed me out. I've never been so stressed out. I've gained like fifty pounds since I started.... Health-wise I'm not in a good space. I've never had problems sleeping. I have problems sleeping. I've just felt exhausted and I can tell the negative impact on my child. He came to me during this last year and said, "Mommy, when are you not gonna be so stressed anymore?"

Jackie tells me about the despair that accompanies so much of the fallout from misogyny.

> My anxiety had definitely gone through the roof. I've been seeing a professional for mental health issues. I was diagnosed with ADHD when I first came into the university at 28—late diagnosis. My needs for talking to people and getting professional help have doubled, basically. I'm on more medication now than I've ever been. I'm still resolute with my work and I absolutely am uncompromising with what I want to talk about and what I want to do and I'm lucky to have a committee that does support me in this. It's just that they're in the minority. They're trying their best even though they're female faculty or queer faculty who are being pushed back against when they're trying to advocate for students. It's incredibly disheartening. There's a current of despair that runs through everything.... I am literally full of anxiety all day, every day. I'm in the process of acquiring a medical card because even though our state has terrible limits and a really, really narrow definition of who's acceptable, I have PTSD now. I've been diagnosed with PTSD and so I qualify and part of that is because of my experiences here.

In *The Body Keeps the Score*, Bessel van der Kolk explains how stress contributes to the kinds of effects my interviewees described.

> Adrenaline is one of the hormones that are critical to help us fight back or flee in the face of danger.... Under normal conditions people react to a threat with a temporary increase in their stress hormones. As soon as the threat is over, the hormones dissipate and the body returns to normal. The stress hormones of traumatized people, in contrast, take much longer to return to baseline and spike quickly and disproportionately in response to mildly stressful stimuli. The insidious effects of constantly elevated stress hormones include memory and attention problems, irritability, and sleep disorders. They also contribute to many long-term

health issues, depending on which body system is most vulnerable in a particular individual. (46)

The insidiousness of misogyny—the refusal of those around you to acknowledge that it exists even while it continues to affect your everyday life—contributes to the kind of stress van der Kolk describes here. Brianna tells me, "In that last year I was at my previous institution, it was very stressful. I don't know if I've experienced that level of stress before, in part because most of it was directed at me and because I and people around me felt targeted." Alyssa tells me about the stress in her life as a result of the misogyny she's experienced:

> It's kinda sad because I love my work and I kinda like academia too—it's nice, the flexibility, the thinking, the intellectual work—but the stress, man. The dreams—I have horrible dreams when these things happen. It literally affects me physically. Thanks to academia, I started therapy. I was thinking, why didn't I start therapy before. We all had stress in our lives all along, but the effects have definitely been stress. I think I tried hard to protect myself from falling behind or not applying for tenure or dropping out of academia. There were moments when I thought, maybe it's not for me, but I worked on keeping my position and keeping my scholarly identity. But again, it's stress and it's anxiety. I know so many women who get sick later on in their lives in academia. So I'm kind of scared of that.

Gwen, too, points to the physical effects of living with misogyny: "I feel like it's contributed to anxiety, exhaustion and fatigue, headaches, so it's impacted my physical health, my mental and emotional health." Eva says, "I'm exhausted all the time and super worried and constantly thinking about if someone hates me... because I'm so anxious all the time, I know it affects my relationship with my boyfriend, my relationship with my mom, my relationship with my dad, with my siblings, and with my friends back home." Patricia tells me,

> I feel like I rocked the boat too much when I got here to be like pal around within the patriarchal system, but I don't really have the mental space or stamina to continue pushing it. It actually got so bad that I was diagnosed with a panic disorder a few years ago, and I've been seeing people and taking meds for that since then, but it's definitely linked to the environment.

Theresa tells me, in reference to the story I shared in Chapter 2 about her male colleague who threw a bomb in the middle of their writing committee, "When all that stuff happened this spring, it was completely traumatizing. I can't even tell you how many nights I lost sleep and how many emails I wrote and how displacing it was of other work, and it was particularly disappointing because I was just coming off my sabbatical and that had been terrific." And Caroline points to the spatial effects of misogynistic trauma:

> It's very physical. People often think that this is just kind of what's happening in our heads, but it's very physical to me. So whenever something like that happens, and I go back to this space—the English department or the classroom—I get a very physical reaction. My heart is pounding, I get sweaty, I feel like I'm gonna throw up, and all these physical reactions. I think it really does things to our bodies because it's also those moments when I pick up colds and flu—our immunity goes down because of all the stress.

Caroline is right that stress does things to our bodies; as van der Kolk explains, when the stress hormones do not return to baseline levels because of chronic stress, our bodies experience sleep disruption, irritability, and, eventually, long-term health issues. Lisa Mosconi confirms this when she writes, "In the short term, too much stress leaves you drained, unhappy, and perpetually overwhelmed. In the long term, it can lead to more serious problems like depression, heart disease, and an increased risk of dementia" (62).

For the first time in her life, Miranda tells me, she has high blood pressure. Some of that is genes, and some of that, she says,

> Let me put it this way. I see the current plight of the humanities as a function of misogyny. The fact that I'm fighting this huge uphill battle even at a liberal arts college that pays lip service to the humanities. Battle for resources and it's a fight for students. I feel like I'm on the defensive all the time, every minute, and I'm trying to be really strategic. I'm trying to persuade my colleagues, you've got to be strategic, you can't just assume that you're gonna last. If you take it back to Bush—we're gonna have a bunch of wars and we're gonna have STEM. This is misogyny in action on a grand scale. It's crippling my students who say, I'll minor in English because I really love it, but I know I can't major. That has had an impact on me personally in a negative way by way of feeling like you're working really hard, but your chances of success are slim.

Misogyny leads to women's anxiety, depression, panic disorders, exhaustion, sleep problems, headaches, and overall stress levels. And it affects women's decisions whether to have children.

Childbearing Decisions

Two women I spoke with told me that the misogyny they'd experienced and witnessed had a considerable effect on their decisions to have or not to have children. Meg tells me,

> It makes me super anxious about having children. When my husband and I first started trying to have a family, we would only try during the months where it would be like, logistically, okay to have an academic baby, and the more I talked to other women about how many people do that, I was just flabbergasted.... I don't mind sharing this, we had a miscarriage, and we've been trying for years, and now I'm like, gosh, we should've just tried. It has these real impacts. When I saw my friend being shamed for the way she was asking for her children to be accommodated, I saw another friend who had a job offer and a negotiation she just brought up her children and I was always coached by other women *not to* and she didn't want to be hired by a place that didn't respect her children, but anyway, they withdrew her offer and we don't know if that was exactly it, but it probably played a role. So I see these things about child/family life and caretaking and I think that it translates—my professional experience does translate to stress in those parts of my life as well.

Meg is not alone. Patricia, too, has likely decided not to have any more children after her experience with her department following her first maternity leave.

> I had wanted a second child, I wanted to do it before I was forty, and I just don't see it in the cards right now because things are still tenuous. Like I said, we have a new chairperson in July, and I don't want to commit to anything until I know what the climate is gonna be like. I can't have a maternity leave like I had last time. We have no policy in place for who takes over the classes and no oversight, and so basically there's a warm body who shows up to your class and you're expected to do all the grading when you get back. It is so much work and it's not even neutral. You're definitely in trouble for it. I'm not the only one who's experienced it. The other woman in my department who had a child around that time also experienced it. There's no way of predicting. It could be fine, it could also not be. I definitely feel like I got mommy tracked.

What's interesting about both Meg and Patricia's reflections on having or not having children is that they notice the way women around them are being treated as well. The misogyny is not just directed at them; it is systemic. There are no policies in place, Patricia notes, for who will take over classes. This leads to more work for a new mother, and "you're definitely in trouble for it."

Effects on Women's Work

Miranda tells me that the misogyny she's experienced in her department has been in some ways good for her work.

> In my graduate education, I had very little feminist anything because it wasn't there to be had, so when I started my career, I was hired because I said I could teach a class on women and literature. So then I had to learn. Never tell somebody you can't teach a class. It was called Women and Literature—so I'd say I learned a lot and it certainly had an impact on the way I approach my scholarship.... It certainly has shaped my teaching—I've taught feminist theory and all kinds of things. Most recently, I taught a course on gender and genre in 19th century British lit—senior seminar and that was fun.

Eva, too, has seen positive outcomes on her scholarship. "I will say it's definitely pushed me to work harder, which sucks because I hate that motivation factor." Eva says her experiences have pushed her to ask the hard questions in her work: "What are the things that are the hardest things for me to look at? That's where my best work comes from. It sucks and I'm exhausted all the time, but I'm doing really cool things in spite of it."

Miranda and Eva are the outliers, though. For many of the women I spoke with, the misogyny they'd experienced in their work lives has led to self-doubt, a lack of confidence, and an inability to tend to their scholarship in ways they would have liked to. As we saw in the chapter on gaslighting, and as Kate Abramson points out in her foundational article on gaslighting, "it's part of the structure of sexism that women are supposed to be less confident, to doubt our views, our beliefs, reactions, and perceptions, more than men" (22). And, as we saw in Chapter 3, respect, authority, and leadership are masculine-coded goods that women are punished for taking or even asking for. So when Lisa tells me that she experiences imposter syndrome, it makes perfect sense.

> I think all people who are new in academia, as I still think of myself as being, deal with imposter syndrome—this idea that I somehow got here by luck. I think that's highlighted even more when there's experiences like Dr. Jones and Dr. Smith and Lisa. It's this idea that, if I were getting the same respect given

naturally to my male colleagues, maybe my imposter syndrome wouldn't be so hard to deal with, you know?

Angela, too, tells me, "I definitely have self-doubt. There is no question that there is a level of self-doubt that I'm working through." Erika says that one of the biggest effects for her was that it "was a long road to being sure that—coming to know my intellectual work and myself as a scholar as kind of separable from those kinds of experiences." Caroline doubts her own agency as an academic, she tells me.

> Am I even going to be heard? Is my research going to matter? Am I talking to a wall? I know that I'm being heard by other women. It is heard. That's exactly what the oppressor does to you—to make you feel like you don't matter.... I see the struggle of being a woman in academic space no matter who you are, no matter how much power you have. Some professors are tenured, but still doubted, their academic voices. When is this going to end? It's both physical and intellectual harm.

Diane addresses what she understands to be others' misogyny toward her work on video games—an area of English Studies that she calls "very male heavy"—by being prepared for questions. "I always have an attitude whenever I do video game work that I need to go in getting ready to answer one or two annoying questions on what are my capabilities, what are my justifications."

The self-doubt transfers to the classroom as well. Gwen tells me,

> It's affected my confidence in the classroom. I don't have the energy. I feel like the climate in the country has changed in a very negative way and I have simply not had the energy to combat that stuff in the classroom. I just don't have it. It's really not cool. It's not good. But if I can't drag myself up to be able to make it, it means my teaching is suffering, it means that the learning is suffering.

Marie describes a different kind of self-doubt that affects her teaching:

> Within my classroom, there's a definite effect of this expectation of a female teacher and this idea that a woman is supposed to be a certain way—nurturing or caring—and if she's not those things. I feel like if a male professor is demanding and rigorous, then they're doing their job, and I feel like if a female professor is those things, she's a bitch. I think those things definitely play into my teaching, and I've noticed more specifically at this institution more than at any other institution, the student evaluations are weighed heavily. I know in my head, I'm

always thinking, how is this going to come across to my students? How are they going to perceive this? How is this gonna change my evaluation? And I *hate* that. I hate that because it's a disservice to my students that I would change my teaching because of those things and I know it and yet, I'm contingent faculty and there's a point where I just need…I need to keep my job. I know a female faculty member who had those sort of comments that we all hear about on evaluations about what she was wearing and the style of clothes. I can't imagine a man is ever gonna get that.

Earlier in this chapter, I quoted Rebecca saying that as a result of the misogyny she's experienced, her scholarship is down. This is perhaps the most visible effect of misogyny on women's work lives: productivity drops. Lillian, too, experienced this.

When I was WPA, I had a length of time—I had a few things in the pipeline and they came out—in terms of publications, but I didn't have a lot coming out in those years because I was just—I'm not one of those folks who can do everything and I had a young son at the time, too, and that was my priority and doing my job as best as I could at the time. I put my research and writing on the back burner. I think that that, in retrospect, maybe didn't have to happen that way for me, but I'm still not sure.

Meg describes the burnout she experienced as a graduate student.

I've definitely experienced burnout. I think the lack of having people when I was a graduate student on my committee to really push my ideas—their inability—and in part, chosen inability—because there are totally male scholars who do great feminist work—if I have a committee member who doesn't understand why feminist theory is useful for me to discuss race, well, that's gonna be not only frustrating but intellectually stagnating. So I think the impact was, one, I think I would have published more if I had had better support. I think that it also dates the education that I and a lot of other graduate students had in the department because they're having us read Bitzer instead of Anzaldua and we have to find it on our own…. Two, the market—you have to be so competitive. I think it also translated to burnout on the market. I mean, it took me seven years to do my Ph.D. Burnout, burnout, burnout.

Amanda is not writing at all anymore. "I have almost no passion left for doing my own creative writing, which is something I've talked about a lot in therapy, and I think the conclusion my therapist and I have come to is that it doesn't feel like it's safe for me to do anything like risk-taking here, and creative writing for me is risk-taking." And Gwen tells me,

> In my scholarship, I've had difficulty writing anyway because of the kinds of things that are being said. I find them so diminishing and disheartening. It hurts my feelings as a human being that this is how people are behaving toward one another, but then it's like the impact, it feels like my work is not appreciated in the department itself. The impact is that it makes me want to leave and follow some of my colleagues who have left. It's made me think about, do I want to be in the academy at all.

Gwen's thinking progresses from not being able to do her scholarship to wondering if she even wants to be in the academy at all. Among the women I spoke with, Gwen is not alone, as we will see below.

But before we get to that, I want to share what two more women told me about the impacts on their work. Jeanne, a doctoral student, told me that she had considered, for a time, switching her field of study from the one she was in to rhetoric and composition, and Jill, an associate professor, told me that because she did not want to be involved with the writing program after the bait-and-switch she tells us about in Chapter 3, she redirected her research to the medical humanities.

Disengaging with Departments

"I come in and I do my work and I leave," Patricia tells me. This is one of the effects of a misogynistic workplace. Women disengage from the culture of their departments, and they stop wanting to give. Patricia continues, "I'm tired of fighting to do my job because it feels like at every step I have to push to show up. I feel like, especially the males, not only is their way clear, but somebody holds the door open for them." Theresa puts it this way: "I think it feeds into a lot of the emotional connection that we have to our workplaces and then can displace, distract, appropriate the space you'd have to do other kind of work." Elizabeth tells me, "I find myself not wanting to engage as much in the department because as an adjunct, I have the choice not to. I don't have to be a part of the committee, I don't have to come to department meetings, I don't have to engage in that environment at all times as an adjunct, so I find myself choosing not to because it's just exhausting to be there."

Laura tells me a story about how she learned to establish boundaries.

> [My experiences with misogyny] have taught me that I can't let school and research and writing take up all of my life and when I got here it was doing that, quite frankly. I was thinking about my first semester and I was laughing to myself because I remember one day I had a fifteen-minute break that I had scheduled for myself and I had just moved into my apartment and I had never gotten a mango before. So, I cut open this mango, it took fifteen minutes and then I was done with my break and I was like, well, I guess I'm done with my free time for the day.

After more time in the department, Laura realized she couldn't allow her work to take up her entire life that way. She tells me, "In order for me to go into these spaces and to hold these silences and to draw lines, I have to have something else inside of me. The thing that I have found that has given me the strength to do that is yoga. I have become a yoga teacher."

"It's made me kind of bitter to the point now where when stuff happens, I roll my eyes and huff out loud, and that's not appreciated," Sara tells me about her experiences with misogyny. And Michelle tells me, "I don't want to say yes in this department."

Eventually, the disengagement becomes so stark that women leave. And this is where we're truly missing out. Women leave because they don't want to put up with the misogyny anymore. About her time in her previous position, Brianna says,

> I think by the time I left that last place, I had thought, do I care enough about being in this field and doing this very specific job that I would stay at a place where this is happening? Would I rather just leave if I can't find a job somewhere else? I think that's sort of one of the consequences—how many women leave instead of dealing with it.

Brianna is one of the women who left her job, though she remains in the academy, in a position that so far has been less difficult than the one she left.

Following Up with Women Who Left

In summer, 2021, I followed up with three women who left their jobs. Susan left her job in the West for another academic job in the East, and Molly and Amanda left academia altogether. All three are experiencing less misogyny in their lives now.

Susan told me that having the distance to reflect on her time at her previous institution helped her realize just how bad it had gotten while she was there. Sometimes, it seems, it takes telling the story to realize how egregious your situation is.

> As I reflect back on my life at my previous institution, I realize how much time and effort, emotional time as well, was spent dealing with all this, and I really felt like there were times that I was kind of depressed and I felt like I just wasn't good enough or I wasn't a good enough teacher, and when I really think about it, it wasn't, I mean, not to be a narcissist, but I like to consider myself a relatively good teacher in the world, knowledgeable about what I am doing, right? But I really found myself questioning what I was doing and who I was as a person and my teaching styles, and I realize a lot of that had to do with the misogyny that I was experiencing around me, so there was a lot of emotional stress all the time.

Like many other women I spoke with, Susan tells me that she now sees that the misogyny she experienced affected her productivity, and it took away time from her son.

> I often felt in that department that I didn't have the right to say no to things, and I think part of that is that I was led to believe that I was already in a deficit position being the woman in the department and being new and being a single mom.... I think when I interviewed with you, I was teaching like ten classes and with pressure to teach more and a lot of them were new. That semester I had nine different classes, only one repeat. Five were ones that had never been taught before. I had been hired to create them.... Looking back on it, they didn't think I could do it or I felt like I had to prove that I could do it and I couldn't be like, hey, nine different classes and ten classes total is way too much for a normal human being. Students are going to suffer, etc. I didn't feel like I ever had the option to say no.

Being on the job market during the time of our initial interview made Susan aware of the misogyny that other women were experiencing on search committees and helped her steer clear of certain departments. "I was like, oh heavens, run, run, run!" At her current institution, Susan is rewarded rather than punished for her knowledge of online teaching, which was of course a boon during the pandemic. Recall from Chapter 4 that Susan was accused of grooming her two male coworkers while helping them learn to teach online. Here, at her new school, "Covid very much helped them see, oh, maybe it'd be a good idea to have someone who understands online education." While her new department is not free of misogyny, Susan tells me that the misogyny she witnesses comes mostly from the fact that it is a religious institution, and though the nuns are mean, "they're not misogynistic mean." After leaving her former institution, Susan published six articles in a year. "My brain is alive! That was a lot! That wasn't just because the number of classes went down. I think it was also getting out of an abusive environment." And the best part is that Susan *sounded* better as I talked to her; we laughed a lot as we recalled some of the stories she'd told me two years earlier, like the one about the coworker who took the job because the department was mostly men and he told Susan that "there's just something about men who talk about literature that's more exciting than when women do." Misogyny is so often absurd, it helps to remind ourselves.

When I talked with Molly two years later, she told me more about her decision to leave academia.

> What pushed me over the edge to make that decision was I came home one day, something frustrating had happened, I don't even remember what now, and I was talking to my partner about it, and after I had kind of unloaded everything, he just said, "You need to find another line of work," and I just laughed. And he was like, "No, I really think it would be good for you to consider another line of work." It was almost like I had never even really considered that there were other things that I was qualified to do that wouldn't make me feel like that every day.

In a way similar to Susan's realizing she was living with misogyny only after she and I talked about misogyny, Molly had never considered doing something other than working in academia until her partner suggested doing something other than working in academia.

> He said it so plainly. It was like, I had a tenure-track position and I was running a writing program—that was the goal. And I was like, well, I got to the goal, I would be a fool to give it up because of these things that happen to me every day.

Molly points to a kind of defeatism that set in when she began her job on the tenure track.

> It's like, this is what you asked for. The struggles are because this is a difficult life, and this is the life you picked. After I left and made it public that I did, I had so many people that I knew, some of whom are still in academia, some of whom are not, reach out to me and be like, tell me how you did it. Tell me what I need to do. What did you do? Where did you look for a job? It just seems so far-fetched when you're in it to actually do it. I literally felt like I was qualified for nothing else.

Molly found a career counselor and eventually found a job in the private sector. "In the work that I do now," she says, "I rarely ever encounter what I would consider misogyny in the way that I did almost daily in my work as a professor." When I ask her about how the pandemic has affected her experienced with misogyny, she tells me,

> Because I'm one of those people who enjoys working from home, it's actually that disconnect from others that has kind of made it subside even more, I think. Not having eyes on me in the same way that going in to an office building does has been actually quite refreshing, to be honest.

About the effects of having left academia, Molly says,

> There's just been such a difference in my wellbeing and mental health from leaving academia and not having to deal with that misogyny is a pretty large part of why. I was in a place where I was so stressed out, my health was so—my physical health was so terrible, I was literally losing my sight. I was diagnosed with a condition where potentially I could have gone blind and stress is a huge contributing factor to that and now—I just went to my ophthalmologist three weeks ago and most of the swelling and all of the things that were going wrong are pretty much gone. It's just been a huge shift for me in physical and mental health and in mindset and future outlook and everything. It was a good decision, and to say, I don't really have to deal with that much misogyny anymore, is a huge statement after dealing with it so frequently for so many years.

Molly wants others to know that, if a job in academia doesn't work out, "you are qualified to do other things. You *are* qualified."

When I spoke with Amanda in 2019, she was finishing up her third year in her doctoral program. When I spoke with her in 2021, she had completed her Ph.D. and had decided to leave academia altogether. Though she was offered an academic job, "the only thing tempting about it was the money." It was a heavy workload, it was far away from family and friends, and "I was just really burnt out and tired of everything from my experiences in my department. So I did find that job, but I started applying for other jobs and went looking for something that had better work/life balance."

Though there were many things that affected her decision not to continue with a career in academia, Amanda tells me that one of the biggest factors was her inability to get feedback on her writing from her dissertation committee.

> At the time the pandemic started, I had written the first four of five chapters of my dissertation, and I had not managed to get my committee to give me feedback on any of them. And I knew my advisor had been giving feedback to other people on their dissertations in the meantime. A guy that he was a reader for, he gave feedback to immediately, and he had my stuff for months and months and months. It just got to this point where it was like, if it's this hard to get respect and the things that I need and I'm not even a faculty member, do I really want a career lifetime of that? And I didn't.

When she did finally defend her dissertation, Amanda had been working in the private sector for about a month and a half.

> It was surreal to come together with these people who said really, really nice things about my work and did not—they asked challenging questions but not questions that led me to believe that they strongly doubted the foundation of my work or anything like that, but I was like, this is what I wanted all along and you never gave it to me. It was all I could do to get you guys to show up for this and it was literally on the last day that I could defend that semester.

One of the most devastating effects for Amanda is, as I mentioned earlier in this chapter, that she no longer writes.

> There were just so many times that the feedback that I got on my writing was really gendered and then to have my dissertation pretty much ignored until I put my foot down and said, hey, I want to graduate by this date, we're gonna make this happen, you've ignored my stuff for a year. That also just told me that my work and my writing had very little value to anybody other than me. And obviously, I shouldn't internalize that too much because my writing can still have value and can still be important, but it's just not a thing I feel like I can do anymore. It sort of feels like the desire to write got beaten out of me a little bit.

At her new job, Amanda doesn't experience the same kind of misogyny that she did when she was a graduate student. In fact when I asked her about experiences with misogyny in the workplace, she told me,

> I would say that they are mostly gone. It's not really a part of my life anymore and that feels amazing. It's not something I experience coming at me from students anymore. Sometimes I get it from people that are outside my company that I speak to for work, but it's not something that I experience from within my company ever. There's no gendered workload expectations or those sort of unspoken

but totally still enacted-upon-you ways that your behavior is assessed and all that. It's just not a thing that I experience anymore. It's such a relief, honestly.

Remarkably, when I asked Amanda how she would respond to misogyny should she experience it in her current work setting, she told me that she would feel much more confident identifying it and reporting it because the experience would not be muddled by anything like the English department's discourse on diversity, equity, and inclusion. "I wouldn't have to go to others in my department and say, 'Is this happening to you, too?'" She would *know* that it was happening to her.

Reflecting on the differences between her time in her Ph.D. program and her life now, working full-time in a position that does not inundate her with misogyny, Amanda says,

> It's this noise in the background of your life all the time that takes your attention away from other things that you could be doing and accomplishing because you're spending time just trying to manage the effects of misogyny in your work life. And then if you couple that with misogyny that exists in your daily life, just existing in our culture, yeah, it does take away from your ability to do other things. It made it, for me at least, much more likely that I would get home and just sort of check out and not do other things that I enjoyed because I didn't feel like I had the bandwidth for it. I feel like I aged so much in the time I was in my Ph.D. program and not just because of the work—I found the work itself really fulfilling and exciting and interesting. It was the social interactions and expectations that really dragged me down. That's one of the things that tells me things are better now—that I'm in a different field—I feel lighter now. I feel like I can just leave my work at work at the end of the day and go do other things, and I'm not rehashing things all the time. I feel freed in many ways. I feel like I can do other things that make me happy.

Amanda's language here is so telling. She feels lighter, she feels freed, she is not rehashing things all the time—and she is thus no longer hypervigilant.

Interestingly, even with my experiences with misogyny in the academy and my experience working for corporations earlier in life, I believed—and I imagine others share this belief—that misogyny would be far more prevalent in a corporate setting than in an academic setting. I imagine that this belief stems from the discourse I'm surrounded by regularly in my department and in my field. But Moira told me that her first real experiences of misogyny in the workplace happened in academia, not in the corporate contexts she worked in before.

I went back to graduate school late in my career and worked for a health sciences corporation for a number of years before that and I was working in grant writing and admin related stuff, and all of the women I worked with there had a lot of stories to tell and maybe I wasn't paying attention, but I didn't have a lot of issues while I was there. So my first real experiences of the sort of misogyny that I'm describing were actually in academic contexts.... The environments I was working in before grad school were academic, but they were also corporate and when I stepped into grad school, I stepped into a more, I don't want to call it pure, but a *more* academic context, an actual academic context, and that's where I first really started to think, "Wow, this is real and this is a problem."

Jeanne told me, too, about her friend who works in a corporation. "She's like, Jeanne, this would never fly. I'd get fired." And Pam told me that her son works for a large health insurance company and told her, "I don't think anyone would get away with that kind of sexual harassment." We in the academy may believe that we are progressive, that we are rooting out the injustices of the world, and we often like to believe that our workplaces are more progressive than the corporations so many of our friends and families work for. But, as Lillian put it,

> I think we all want to feel like the profession to which we've devoted so much time and energy is above certain kind of frays because we've made so many sacrifices, but that's just not the case. That's just not the case. It's as bad, if not worse, in the university, as it is anywhere else. And maybe worse because we've got egos and ostensible intellects involved who have the wherewithal, the intellectual capacities to make things worse in some ways. That's a disappointment, but it's also—I think it's once you sort of get through the disappointment, it's a healthy sort of realization because it takes the university off of that pedestal.

I think hearing from Molly and Amanda helps us take the university off that pedestal, too. One thing that stuck with me about my 2019 interview with Amanda was that she said, "If, for some reason, I couldn't have this career anymore, I would just move on because it's been horrible anyway, and I would just find a way to carry on with my life." And she did. She knocked the university off its pedestal and she carried on with her life in a position that allows her a much better work/life balance and does not include misogynistic treatment.

What we know but what others need to know: As a result of systemic misogyny in English departments, women get sick, women disengage in their departments, their productivity suffers, and they think about leaving. Sometimes they do leave. And sometimes their minds are on it for a very long time. "I really almost quit every single day for the last year and a half," Jody told me. Women understand that it's not just about them, too. They wonder, as Gwen does, "How can we in good conscience recruit?" How can we actively bring other women into these departments that grind us down and make us sick?

References

Abramson, Kate. "Turning Up the Lights on Gaslighting." *Philosophical Perspectives* 28 (2014): 1–30.
Mosconi, Lisa. *The XX Brain*. New York: Avery, 2020.
van der Kolk, Bessel. *The Body Keeps the Score*. New York: Penguin, 2014.

7

Less Precarious Stories

> Having names for problems can make a difference. Maybe before, you could not quite put your finger on it. With these words as tools, we revisit our own histories; we hammer away at the past.
>
> —Sara Ahmed, "Evidence"

I have not been able to share all of the stories women shared with me. In this concluding chapter, I want to tell you a few more. I want to tell you about Patricia's chair lying in wait for her to make a mistake.

> I had documentation that my email server wasn't working and that I had IT working on it, and my chair sent me an email and I didn't respond. It was flagged with a read receipt but it was never read. Then the dean sent me an email and it was never read because I have IT working on this. They wait for four days before they write me up for not responding to official email, and when I show them the documentation that my email was down, they're like, you should have told us. And I'm like, I'm sorry, why didn't you tell me to check my email because there's an email waiting for me, then I could have told you it was broken. They're like, we shouldn't have to do that. It just became this huge, huge issue. All it should have been was—I'm across the hall from the chair—did you get my email? No, my email's down. But it just became this thing where they were kind of lying in wait for me.

I want to tell you about the male graduate student who really wanted Laura's book.

> It was maybe my second week in the Ph.D. program. We were given books by the department to welcome us here. There was a big collection of books. I first and foremost identify as a feminist scholar. That's what I'm doing, that's why I'm here. There was a book on feminism and food, so I grabbed the book in a way that might have been aggressive, I don't know, but I had a right to it. I wasn't shoving anybody, it was there. Come and take them. So I take the book and then later in my office, one of the male students comes, closes the door, and we're chatting for a few minutes… and I've known him for a couple weeks… we were not close. He looks at my bookshelf once he's been in my office and says, "I really wanted that book," but before that, he said, "I don't really identify as a feminist, I don't get

that. I don't understand why everyone's talking about feminism so much here, like, I'm not on board." And then he's like, "But I want that book because at the college I used to teach at we had classes on food and I would like to teach one and I want to know more about that." And I said, "Maybe I'll let you borrow it after I read it," and I would not give it to him, and I could see that he was becoming very red in the face and mad that I would not give him my book, the book that he could have theoretically taken that I got for free but he instead got a different book.

It's hard not to notice in Laura's telling the way she has internalized the misogynistic judgment of having possibly been aggressive and/or shoving when she grabbed the book that was offered to her. My guess is that that language would not have appeared in her story if the male graduate student had not later expressed his sense of entitlement to her book.

I want to tell you what Lucy told me she overheard.

I once overheard a conversation—I swear I wasn't snooping—when I heard them talking about a colleague of mine. They said she wouldn't know research if it hit her in the head, and the thing is she's really smart, she's in a Ph.D. program, she's almost done, she got promoted, what else do you want from her to prove herself. So there's nothing left—we'll attack her research ability. That's fine. And that's the department head who said that.

I want to share with you what Theresa observed about women delivering feminine-coded goods.

I see it happening a lot where people will be walking the halls and bump into people and it feels like people often get stalled and then deliver some of that empathy, standing and listening to someone's complaints about their own work or about something that happened, and I see that happening a lot across rank.

And I wanted to share with you what Caroline said about microaggressions.

I don't like the term microaggression because it sounds like it's micro, so small, but if you are already so burned, even a little touch will feel excruciating. It's also like smoking—you feel like you get this harm, but it's okay, I don't feel anything different, but after a while, you get cancer.

I want to share these moments and observations with you because, while they aren't all stories in the traditional sense, they all point to an understanding of the ways women are expected to give of themselves without expecting anything in return. They are stories and moments that stuck with me after I spoke with my interviewees. I want these stories, these moments, these observations, to serve as narrative resources for the women who come after, for the women who are reading this work, as they begin to shape their own stories.

In her essay, "A Cure for Bitterness," Dorothy Allison captures the importance of witnessing our stories on the page. She writes, "If I live in a world in which my experience is not reflected back to me, then maybe I'm not real enough; maybe I'm not real at all. Maybe I'm fiction." One of the reasons I began this project was to help others see themselves on the page; I am confident that the stories I've shared in this book are stories that women in English departments across this country can relate to and can recognize themselves in. To put it in the negative, not seeing our experiences reflected back to us in the literature is, as Allison says, a trauma. "That is a trauma: to see yourself never in the world. To feel yourself so unspeakable, forbidden, dangerous" (246). Women in English departments who experience misogyny share stories with one another in confidence; they participate in the whisper network, surely. But perhaps they haven't yet named their experiences as misogyny.

Misogyny is the law enforcement branch of patriarchy. It punishes women who violate the norms that tell us that we are here to give feminine-coded goods and that men are entitled to take masculine-coded goods. When we err in our roles as givers, we are punished with any number of down-girl moves. Misogyny is not the hatred of all women; it is the inability to allow women space outside their roles as givers. When we begin to understand misogyny in this way, our stories become newly interpretable. This is my hope.

When I was young, I was the victim of sibling abuse by my older sister. I did not have the concept of sibling abuse until I was in my twenties, but I experienced the abuse all throughout my childhood and into my teenage years. When I finally learned the term, when I learned that there were people who took this kind of abuse seriously, I felt seen and understood in a way I never had before. I felt witnessed. I felt able to begin telling my story. And I've been telling that story in a number of ways since. Because I want other survivors of sibling abuse to understand that it is real, that is it not sibling rivalry, and that it has far-reaching consequences. While I recognize that there are many who will read these stories and respond by critiquing the very belief that we can ever know another person's experience by way of their telling a story, I'm more interested in what Ann Jurecic calls "ordinary motives for reading and writing" (3). Jurecic writes of contemporary literary criticism that

> Distrust of texts' errors, lies, and manipulations has become prescriptive, and the project of much contemporary criticism has become to anticipate and contain textual and theoretical problems in advance. For scholars trained in such habits of reading, the idea of trusting a narrative to provide access to the experience of another person indicates a naïve understanding of how such texts function. Before a contemporary critic begins to read an autobiography about cancer or pain, she knows that it has been constructed by medical discourse and political, economic, and social forces. She also knows that common readers are likely to misread it because they will assume they can try on the experience of the author and that they will therefore succumb to the myriad powers of dominant discourse. (3)

I know that this criticism exists, but frankly, I'm not interested in it. Instead, what I'm interested in is the power of storytelling to reveal aspects of our lives that we haven't yet shone light on. As a teacher and practitioner of life writing, I'm more inclined to Allison's interpretation of the popularity of memoir.

> Memoir is canonized and popularized in part, I believe, by our worst impulses, our lust for gossip. But in part also by what I think of as one of our best impulses. We want a correction to lies. We want to know what is true. We want our lives and our true lived experience to be taken seriously. (246)

We want a correction to the gaslighting. These stories are not one-offs. They happen again and again with slight modifications for time and place and the people involved. Women learn to write these experiences off, to downplay them, to explain them away, and they hear again and again from others in their departments that, well, "That's just how he is." The number of times I heard this during my interviews was shocking to me—perhaps it shouldn't have been, but it was. That's just how he is. And that's precisely the problem.

*

One of the effects I did not mention in Chapter 6 is that women internalize the misogyny they're exposed to. Refusing the norms of the patriarchy is not as simple as choosing to do so; they are a part of us. In her essay, "Thank You for Taking Care of Yourself," Melissa Febos quotes her friend Ada when she compares patriarchy to a virus. "It was an apt comparison. Like a virus, patriarchy harms the systems it infects and relies on replication to survive. It flourishes in those who are not aware of its presence, and sometimes even in those actively working to expel it" (217).

In Chapter 1, we heard from Patricia, who told us that she feels like she is "slowly acquiescing to that shock collar. I no longer want to have ideas at meetings. I sit in meetings and I'm so quiet. I just try to barrel through them." She also told me that the department culture is such that women "don't trust each other because we recognize that it's a bit more cutthroat for us and so it becomes even more confrontational with the other women in the department." Two other women I spoke with pointed to such internalized misogyny as an effect of living with misogyny in their work lives.

Alexandra, referring to a weeks-long listserv discussion on the WPA listserv (now no longer live) about misogyny and racism on the list, says, about graduate students who participated in that discussion,

> I'm thinking about all the stuff that went down on the WPA listserv this fall. And I had so much anxiety for them—are you gonna be able to get a job after tweeting like this? That is wrong. These people should be able to talk about this experience and call out the b.s. and my response should not be, are you gonna be able to get a job after this? And yet, at the same time, I had that fear for them. We have to stop that.

Alexandra goes back and forth here, worrying about graduate students' reputations and realizing that she shouldn't have to worry about their reputations. In a just world, she wouldn't have to. But women who speak out against misogyny are subject to more misogyny, and Alexandra knows this and could feel herself both judging the graduate students' responses and judging her judgment. She was fighting her internalized misogyny.

Meg put it most directly when she was talking with me about her struggles to capture what it feels like to live with the effects of misogyny.

> I don't have all the words for it, but I want to acknowledge that I also think that these experiences have led me to internalize misogyny even though I was raised by academics who write about things like this. I'm set up in so many ways not to have—but it's inevitable. The last thing I want to put out into a project like this is that one consequence of these experiences socially but also professionally is that there's no reprieve, and our professional spaces should offer a reprieve, and when they don't we internalize them also professionally. Personally, of course, that's gonna happen because that's inevitable, but it's also inevitable when it happens in our professional spaces to then in the categories of our identity that we think of as professional to then also internalize that misogyny. I'm not sure exactly what that looks like in practice in my life, but I know that it's there and that it informs

some of my reactions to things and so I just wanted to acknowledge that I am then also, therefore, complicit.

Our professional spaces should offer reprieve, Meg suggests, from the misogyny of the everyday world, but they do not, and so women internalize that misogyny and likely judge one another according to the norms of patriarchy, as we saw in Chapter 5.

We've seen a number of women express the belief that the academy is supposed to be a space that is, if not free of, then at least a space with a little less egregious misogyny, but again and again, women are disappointed to learn that it is not. The academy's values align with the patriarchy; the difference in English departments is that we claim otherwise, and one of the effects is that women who are treated misogynistically begin to internalize that misogyny.

One way this internalized misogyny came through in the interviews was in women's apologies to me as they spoke. They apologized to me for sounding bitter (women should accept misogyny without complaint), for crying (women should accept misogyny without being hurt), and for being long-winded in their storytelling (women should be audiences rather than speakers.) "Patriarchy," Febos writes,

> is the house in which we all live. It possesses all of Western culture and industry and has for centuries. But I knew what she [Ada] meant, the way that a part of one's mind that one has worked hard to expunge of patriarchal values can suddenly regress. Even the most self-actualized women I know have embedded voices in them still faithful to the power structures they have long intellectually condemned. Unbidden, they pipe up, *Don't eat that!* (217)

I am not so naïve as to believe that sharing these stories in this book will purge the patriarchal values we all have internalized, but I do believe that we can all become a little more aware of our surroundings, that we can share more stories of our experiences in our workplaces, and that we can, in doing so, feel a little bit less alone. That is the power of storytelling. We can also expand our storytelling to share what happened when we called it out.[11] Because knowing better what

11 In her essay, "Seeing Through the Lens of Troublesome Tropes," sociologist Melinda Mills does this: she tells what happens when she shared her experience of sexual harassment with a colleague. Mills' colleague's response was "'You know how he is, always saying something silly. That's just [name.]'" Mills writes that, "In that moment, in that casual, almost indifferent response, I experienced a different but

misogyny is can help us identify it and call it out. But I also recognize that this is not always possible, for I am well aware of how misogyny works. Manne tells us again and again that "it's dangerous to call out such misogyny.... This is particularly true for women who dare to complain or even name instances of misogyny that are remotely controversial. Our designated role is that of being moral listeners, not critics or censors" (289–90).

We can also expect more of men without worrying about their motivations for why they do what they do; one of the benefits of Manne's conceptualization of misogyny is that it centers women's experiences and does not require an understanding of the motivations of individual people. People can act misogynistically without intending to or they can act misogynistically with every intention to belittle or humiliate. It's not our job to determine which it is; what can be our job is to *expect more* of men and to let them know that we expect more.

But even more than expecting more of men, we can treat women with respect for the whole beings they are. We can stop looking to them as carers or helpers or givers and instead look to them for their expertise and their leadership, for their knowledge and their experience. But even more than looking to them for these things, we can *give* them more. More authority, more compensation, more care, more loyalty, more space. We can give them these things and we can listen when someone like Patricia says, "I kind of wonder, if I didn't have the ball and chain on, what I could have done these past four years. I do feel like I've been trying to do a triathlon with the old cartoony ball and chain on my ankle. It's the same distance, but I've got more obstacles than you do, and guys *really* don't get that."

References

Ahmed, Sara. "Evidence." *Feminist Killjoys*, 12 July 2016.
Allison, Dorothy. "A Cure for Bitterness." *Critical Trauma Studies*. Ed. Monica J. Casper and Eric Wertheimer. New York: New York University Press, 2016. 244–255.

attendant kind of trauma—the trauma of not being seen, heard, or believed" (25). Though the colleague she confided in had a history of advocating for students who had experienced sexual harassment and assault, Mills learns that she would not receive the benefit of such advocacy. "As faculty, or maybe (and more likely) as a brown woman, my victimization would remain illegible, unintelligible. I could not be seen as a victim, so the encounters of harassment from my colleague I had recounted *had to be* met with indifference" (25).

Febos, Melissa. "Thank You for Taking Care of Yourself." *Girlhood*. New York: Bloomsbury, 2021. 193–269.

Jurecic, Ann. *Illness as Narrative*. Pittsburgh: University of Pittsburg Press, 2012.

Manne, Kate. *Down Girl: The Logic of Misogyny*. New York: Oxford UP, 2018.

Mills, Melinda. "Seeing Through the Lens of Troublesome Tropes." *Me Too, Feminist Theory, and Surviving Sexual Violence in the Academy*. Ed. Laura Gray-Rosendale. New York: Lexington Books, 2020. 13–31.

Index

A

Ahmed, Sara xvi, 21, 94-5, 129

B

Beard, Mary 30, 35, 39-40
boundaries 72-4, 120-1

C

clothing 62-3, 67, 82, 119

E

emotional labor 46, 49-50, 54, 61, 75, 106

F

Febos, Melissa 27, 43, 51, 132, 134
Friedman, Jaclyn 78-9

G

Gilmore, Leigh 22, 78-9
gossip xii, xvii, 1, 2, 9, 17-9, 21, 68, 82, 132
graduate students 4, 14, 15, 20-1, 34-6, 47-8, 54, 61-3, 69, 74, 80, 85-8, 94, 97-100
Graeber, David 2

H

hepeating xii, 23, 30-4, 37, 41

I

isolation 12-13, 20, 85

L

leadership 47, 48, 58-9, 60-2, 66-7, 100

M

mansplaining 33, 36
misogyny, definition 5-8
misogyny, differentiated from sexism 6
mothering 53-4

N

narrative habitus 9-11, 16-7, 20, 25, 75
narrative resources 8-10, 131

P

precariousness 8-11, 14

R

retaliation 4, 20-3, 68, 84
Rose, Jacqueline 91

S

Solnit, Rebecca 1

V

van der Kolk, Bessel 113-15

A BOOK SERIES FOR EQUITY SCHOLARS & ACTIVISTS
Beth Powers-Costello, *General Editor*

Globalization increasingly challenges higher education researchers, administrators, faculty members, and graduate students to address urgent and complex issues of equitable policy design and implementation. This book series provides an inclusive platform for discourse about—though not limited to—diversity, social justice, administrative accountability, faculty accreditation, student recruitment, admissions, curriculum, pedagogy, online teaching and learning, completion rates, program evaluation, cross-cultural relationship-building, and community leadership at all levels of society. Ten broad themes lay the foundation for this series but potential editors and authors are invited to develop proposals that will broaden and deepen its power to transform higher education:

(1) Theoretical books that examine higher education policy implementation,
(2) Activist books that explore equity, diversity, and indigenous initiatives,
(3) Community-focused books that explore partnerships in higher education,
(4) Technological books that examine online programs in higher education,
(5) Financial books that focus on the economic challenges of higher education,
(6) Comparative books that contrast national perspectives on a common theme,
(7) Sector-specific books that examine higher education in the professions,
(8) Educator books that explore higher education curriculum and pedagogy,
(9) Implementation books for front line higher education administrators, and
(10) Historical books that trace changes in higher education theory, policy, and praxis.

Expressions of interest for authored or edited books will be considered on a first come basis. A Book Proposal Guideline is available on request. For individual or group inquiries please contact:

    editorial@peterlang.com

To order other books in this series, please contact our Customer Service Department at:

    peterlang@presswarehouse.com (within the U.S.)
    orders@peterlang.com (outside the U.S.)

Or browse online by series at www.peterlang.com

www.ingramcontent.com/pod-product-compliance
Lightning Source LLC
Chambersburg PA
CBHW061717300426
44115CB00014B/2730